I Love You, Mom

Dr. Carter Brown

Copyright © 2013 Dr. Carter Brown
All rights reserved.
ISBN: **0991967305**
ISBN 13: **978-0991967308**

All rights reserved. No part of this book may be reproduced in any form or by any means without the prior written consent of the author, excepting brief quotes used in reviews.

If you purchased this book without a cover, you should be aware that this book is stolen property. It was reported as "unsold and destroyed" to the publisher, and neither the author nor the publisher has received any payment for this "stripped book."

All Dr. Carter Brown titles are available at special quantity discounts for bulk purchases for sales promotions, premiums, fund-raising, and educational or institutional use. Special book excerpts or customized printing can also be created to fit special needs. For details, write to the office of JD Publishing Company special sales manager: JD Publish Company., #3-422, 4th Street, Estevan, Saskatchewan, S4A 0V1, Canada.

This book is a work of fiction. Names, characters, businesses, organizations, places, events, and incidents either are the product of the author's imagination or are used fictitiously. Any resemblance to an actual person, living or dead, events, or locales is entirely coincidental.

JD Books are published by

JD Publishing Company
#3-422, 4TH STREET
Estevan, Saskatchewan
S4A 0V1 Canada

Mothers are indescribably wonderful. They love us unconditionally, from the very day we entered their womb, and love us even more the first day they set their eyes on us and carry us in their arms.

A special thank you goes out to the Chicago Police Department and the New York Police Department for their marvelous help and efforts in bringing this book to life. I really appreciate you guys for the great insight into law and order.

To Jibril Shaban and John Attrel for always being there

To Joan, Burnice, and Day-the lights of my life
And to my family and friends for their support
              -CB

This book is dedicated to all mothers around the world and is inspired by the deep love and gratitude I feel for mothers everywhere. I love you, and I understand the sacrifices and suffering you go through each day just to make your children happy as they grow up. You feed them, you clothe them, you clean them up, and you play with them just to keep them happy. When your child is sick, you worry as you seek a solution. You worry when your child doesn't eat. You stay up all night when your child is awake and crying. These are just a few of the struggles you go through with selfless affection and care. This world wouldn't have existed without you. May this book be a heartfelt tribute to your tireless sacrifices.

Chapter 1

Sixteen years had passed since his father had died from a tragic heart attack in Chicago. Solomon was now twenty-three years old; he was in college and doing well. His mother, Clare, who was forty-three years old, was so proud of him. Working two jobs as a registered nurse, she provided him with everything he needed so he could realize his parents' dreams for him.

On Mother's Day, a Saturday afternoon, Solomon called his mother into the basement. The basement had a white leather couch sitting in the middle. On the east wall hung a handmade cards, which he carefully design, describing his mother's love for him. He asked her to sit down. She stared at him and then sat down without a word. Solomon took a plastic bag from behind the white leather couch and gave it to her. She sat close, looking at him.

Clare anxiously opened the bag to reveal a bunch of flowers all nicely wrapped together in a bundle. There were roses, irises, sunflowers, and lilies. She smelled the flowers and stared at her son with a wild smile. "Thank you."

Solomon looked in her eyes and replied, "You are my angel and my best friend. Thank you for being my mother; I love you dearly. I've always known that you are a light shining on me, illuminating my dark path, but I turned off that light at a certain point when I thought I was man enough to make my own decisions. I'm sorry for missing last Mother's Day and Thanksgiving. I still have the gifts I bought for you."

He gently took out a little wooden box from his right front jeans pocket and gave it to Clare. His mother opened the little box and saw an eighteen-karat, square (diamond-cut) snake chain inside. Clare took out the chain and read the little card: *I love you, Mom.* She put them back in the box and closed it.

Solomon continued, "No other woman on the face of this earth will ever take your place. In my heart there is a special place where I'm keeping your love, and it will remain untouched until I die.

"Life is not easy; things change, as do the attitudes of people. Many things have changed in my life since I left you, but not a day goes by that I don't think of you.

"I remember when I was a little boy growing up in Chicago; you were very happy and proud of me. You quit your job at the nursing home just to take care of me because you wanted to watch me grow up. When I ran around the house, you followed me closely, making sure I didn't fall, and if I did, you picked me up, and laughed and played with me before telling me to be strong. You loved me so much.

"You were so proud of me—you boasted about me to all of your friends, telling them I was your little angel.

"Every morning, I watched you prepare my lunch for school and make sure my clothes were neat and clean. Whenever I was with you, I felt comfortable and happy.

"You told me great bedtime stories every night. Sometimes late at night, when I was in bed, I would see you standing at my door watching me, making sure I was comfortable enough to sleep well. You and I were so close that sometimes I saw jealousy in my father's eyes. But he was a good father, and I miss him.

"Every morning you thought about me before thinking about yourself. When I got sick, you worried and stayed beside me, praying for me to get well.

"You always thought I was a good boy, and you appreciated everything I did. When I did something wrong in front of others, you protected my name and took me home before asking me to focus on doing good things. You always forgave me when I did wrong, realizing that I was just a kid. You are a great human being, and I will always tell the world about how great a mother you are.

"All the advice you gave me when I was little prepared me to be a man, and it rings in the back of my mind and makes me feel guilty for my bad choices. This has made me decide that I want to prove my love to you so that the pain you endured during my birth was not wasted. I plan to always be by your side."

When Solomon was done speaking, he hugged her and kissed her on the cheek before saying happily, "Happy Mother's Day, Mama."

She stared at him for a moment, taking it all in. Then she spoke. "You make me feel like the world's greatest mother, and I am so lucky to have a son like you." She was shocked and excited at how God was answering her prayers for her son.

***

Solomon was now living in Brooklyn, New York. Everyone talked about how kind Solomon was and how serious he was in college. He told his mother that he wanted to stay in school until he obtained his PhD.

But each day when he watched his mother enduring sleepless nights and threatening letters from banks and bill collectors frightened Solomon. Clare would suddenly get paranoid each time her phone rang, and she would be afraid to pick it up, thinking it might be one of the banks or collection agencies calling for their money.

Eager to help his mother, Solomon decided to give school a break and make money.

Two months later he came home from school one afternoon and saw his mother sitting in the kitchen reading her *Time* magazine. He gently kissed her on the cheek, went into the living room, and sat down on the dark brown leather couch.

Clare's living room was sparsely furnished. It was painted white with a small water fountain made of bamboo, a thirty-two-inch television, a fireplace, and a large painting of Solomon that dominated the east wall. It was tidy and elegant with plenty of space for movement.

"Mom, there's something I want to tell you."

She came over and sat down beside him. "I'm all ears," she said.

"You know, Mom, I love you."

"I don't really know that yet. The only way I'll know for sure that you love me is when you graduate."

Solomon stared at her, looked at the floor, and then asked, "Mom, do you want something to drink?"

"Actually, yes. I was just thinking of a big glass of cold water."

He went to the kitchen and served her a glass of cold water. She sipped it and set it on the table. She glanced at her son eagerly, waiting to hear what he had to say.

"Mom, I won't be able to finish school. I have been thinking about how to get rich for some time now. There's some business I need to take care of in Manhattan. This will make us very rich within a year or so, and then I'll take good care of you for the rest of your life. You won't have to work like this anymore."

"Who are you planning to move to Manhattan with?"

"My friend Ebenezer McClanican; you don't have to worry about anything."

"I didn't tell you I wanted to be rich or to live like a queen. All I ever wanted was for you to go to school and finish what you started. Can't you see that you're now the only man in my life? Remember, this was what your father wanted. I am not going to sit here and listen to you, and I will not kill myself thinking about your stupidity." She got up and went upstairs to her room.

Solomon didn't care. His mind was set on what he wanted to do.

Chapter 2

The next day, when Clare got up, she called Mr. Benson Carter, their family friend, and told him what Solomon had planned to do with his life.

Mr. Carter, a sixty-seven-year-old man with brown eyes, silver hair, and clean white teeth, came to talk to Solomon and beg him to stay in school and finish his education. He told Solomon why everyone wanted him to do this. But Mr. Carter was just wasting his time; Solomon's mind was already made up.

"You know that I'm like your father now. Anything you want to do with your life, I'll still be there for you. I know that your father was a good man, and all he ever talked about was you finishing school to gain the kind of respect he always dreamed about but felt he never had. He wanted you to make us all proud. He died fighting for that, and you want to throw it all away. Call me if you need any help, and I'll be there for you." Mr. Carter walked away and joined Clare in the living room.

Solomon didn't care about his words, just as he hadn't cared what his mom said.

Clare continued to try to convince Solomon to stay in school, but he wasn't interested. "School is not for me; if you want to go back to school, that's fine, but nobody, not even you or Mr. Carter, will force me to change my mind or do something against my will."

"My son, all I want you to do is to think about your father, Derrick, the day he was lying in your arms dying," his mother cried.

The guilt hit Solomon hard, but he just got up and walked to his room.

The next morning, breakfast was ready, and his mother was sitting there waiting. They ate in silence, and then he helped her clear the table and put everything away.

"Come, I want to talk to you," she said. Solomon went over and sat down.

"I was thinking all night about what you said to me yesterday. I just want you to understand that, as your mother, I'll still support you. I believe that you're your own man now, and that you're able to make decisions that you think will benefit you more than what we want for you.

"It's like we are trying to force you against your will, and I don't think that is fair to you."

Solomon was overjoyed. His lips suddenly broadened into a wild smile.

"This has made me very happy. I couldn't do this without your support. I love you, Mom." He hugged and kissed her.

That day Solomon prepared dinner and invited Ebenezer over to eat with them.

"Don't worry, Clare, I'll take good care of your son," Ebenezer told Clare.

"How old are you, Ebenezer?" she asked.

"I'm twenty-three. My birthday was two days ago."

"Let me tell you guys something very important," said Clare with a serious face. "Remember, nothing comes easy in this world. If you want something, you have to work hard for it. You can do anything in life if you put your mind to it. As the two of you are going to work or do business, or whatever it is you're going to do, you have to be fair with each other and love each other. I'll be praying for you, and I hope you can call me every day, if possible.

"What did your parents say to you about quitting school and moving away?" she asked Ebenezer.

"They're fine with it. They are going to pay for our transportation as well as money to help us when we first get there," he replied.

"That's interesting. They really must love you, am I right?"

"Oh yes. I don't let them make any decisions for me. They realize that I'm old enough to make my own choices. That's what I've been doing since I was eighteen."

"You have just one more year to finish college. What makes you think that quitting and moving away is so important?"

"We are young and strong, and we have no more time to waste," Ebenezer said.

"What kind of business are you guys going into?"

"What do you want to know?"

"Everything, I'm just curious."

"I think that will be our secret for now."

Solomon was sitting and listening to them with a smile, thinking about the impression his friend was making on his lovely mother.

"OK, I have to get going now before it gets too late."

"Do you want Solomon to drive you home?"

"No, I'm driving," replied Ebenezer. He said good-bye and left.

"I told you that Ebenezer is a good man. I think he is much better than Jack Epstein, Solomon childhood best friend," said Solomon.

"Well, I don't know about that. I thought you knew Jack to be a good man. Make sure you pack everything in your suitcase before you forget something important. I have an envelope here from Mr. Carter. It's sealed, and I'll give it to you as soon as you're ready." Clare got up and went to her room.

Solomon went into the kitchen and prepared a cup of tea. He was watching television when the phone rang. It was Ebenezer.

"I was calling to tell you that I just got home."

"Thanks for letting me know. I'm just sitting here thinking about how our life will be when we leave here."

"What are you thinking about?"

"I was only thinking that we're going to quit school to go after something bigger, but I am still lost about where we are going, who will be there, and where we will be staying. I don't want to hurt my mother again; she has tried so hard for me."

Solomon continued, "You see, my father died from a heart attack when I was seven years old. My mother had to take on the burden of both parental roles. She is a great mother. On Thanksgiving Day she bought me gifts; she said I gave her hope. She prepared a big turkey dinner, and she watched me take my share and eat before she ate. After dinner she prayed with me and made that celebration a happy one.

"My mother's attitude toward me changed soon after I entered my teen's years; she became very strict. She punished me for everything I did wrong. Her punishment was too much, and I often thought she hated me. I was scared of her; she wanted me to be a good son. She hated bad and loved good. She wanted me to live by those rules.

"As her advisors, my grandparents told her to raise me properly, so that when I grew up, I wouldn't fail them. That is just what my mother was doing with me. I did my homework on time and did everything correctly because I knew what would happen if I didn't. I was smart in school, and my teachers loved me for that.

"One day I asked my mother why she hated me so much. She was stunned by my question. Looking me in my eyes, she came closer to me and said, 'I don't hate you. I love you. In fact, I love you more than I love myself. The first thing I ever think of when I wake up in the morning is what to do to make you smile. I want you to be a man of principle and do the right thing. I don't want you to ever think I hate you.'

"From that day forward, I started noticing the softer side of her, and our communication as mother and son grew even more. She started talking to me as a friend, and this made me love her even more because I was happy to share my secrets with her. We were best friends.

"In school I always thought about money," Solomon continued. "I had hopes of becoming rich someday. When I walked to school, I looked at all the nice houses, fast cars, and well-dressed people, and I thought of how great their lives were. I wanted to experience that. I wanted to have money so I could take my mother out of poverty. The only idea my mother had at the time to help me achieve my goal was obtaining the best education.

"She bought me books and took me to various workshops to listen to motivational speakers. I started reading and writing every thought that came to my mind, but whenever I read what I had written, I realized that all my thoughts pertained to money.

"One afternoon my mother took me to a supermarket to meet with the owner, Mr. Nolan Montgomery. Without talking, my mother gave him my notes. He took them and quickly read them. He looked at me and paused for a moment before saying, 'Life is not that easy, but you are a handsome young man with strong determination. I don't think you'll get too far before your dreams come true.' He paused and stared at me.

"'Mr. Montgomery' I said, 'what is the meaning of what you've just told me?'

"'I'm simply telling you that you have lots of hard work to do to make your dreams happen. You'll have to be very patient and work hard to make your dreams a reality.' He stood up, shook my hand, and wished me good luck. When I was about to open his office door, he called my name and told me to chase my dreams until I caught them."

Solomon paused before adding, "I have been chasing my dreams ever since, but I've felt like a man lost in the darkness until I met you."

"Solomon, I don't want you to worry about anything at all," Ebenezer said. "We are going to stay with my brother. After we learn all about the business and are ready to work by ourselves, we'll get our own place. I know you'll like it there. I want you to think big and believe in yourself. Do you know why my brother became a millionaire? He always had faith that he would be rich one day. He left home at an early age and worked with his friends. He established his own contacts before he started on his own. It was tough, but he made it. I picked you as a partner because you're a likable person, and I know I can't make it alone."

"You know, each time I ask you about what we are going to do and what kind of business it is that we are going into, you never give me an answer. Is it because you don't want me to know about it until we get there or what?"

"It's not that I don't want to tell you exactly, Solomon, but it's not right for me to explain everything to you at this point. I've told you a lot about what we are going to do already. There are sensitive issues that we shouldn't talk about, especially on the phone. Look, we are leaving the day after tomorrow, so I want you to get ready and don't look back." Ebenezer said good night and hung up the phone.

Chapter 3

Clare woke up Solomon the next morning, and he went to prepare breakfast. Before long, Ebenezer and his family arrived, and Clare welcomed them. Shortly thereafter breakfast was ready, and she called them to come to the table. They bowed their heads, Clare said a short prayer, and they ate.

Afterward both parents gave words of encouragement before holding hands and praying together. Their parents escorted Ebenezer and Solomon to the train station to see them off. From that day Clare and Ebenezer's parents became friends.

Solomon and Ebenezer caught the train for Manhattan.

"Why couldn't your brother just share his riches with you?" Solomon asked.

"My brother has always been like that, even when we were little. He wanted me to work for my money. He never gave me money without working for it. He told me never to trust any man because the person you trust is the one who will send you to jail. The only thing he did was pay my tuition fees."

"It's good to know that he cares about you. I'm happy to know that we are going to see someone who cares about our success," said Solomon.

When they arrived Ebenezer's brother was waiting for them at the station.

"My name is Andy, and you guys are welcome at my house." Andy was a skinny, six-foot-tall, thirty-three-year-old gentleman, with dark hair, brown eyes, and a light complexion.

"You'll be staying here with me for now." He took one of his business cards and gave it to Solomon. "Now you guys are in Manhattan, where everything is fast."

At Andy's home they freshened up, and Andy took them to his favorite restaurant where they had a great time, eating, drinking, and swapping stories. Andy dropped them off at home and went to his appointment.

While they were sitting there talking, a knock sounded at the door. Ebenezer opened it, and Andy was standing there.

"I thought you had a spare set of keys for your apartment," Ebenezer said.

"No. I only had one set, and I left those with you guys," he said as he came in and locked the door. He took out a roll of cash from his front right pocket and set it on the table.

"You know why I wanted you guys to come and stay here in Manhattan?"

"No," they replied.

"I want you guys to take over my business because I will be retiring."

"Why do you want to retire now?" Solomon asked.

"Well, Solomon, I'm now thirty-three. I have a son on the way, and I don't want to be greedy. I've made enough money; I'm now set for life. It's time to make someone else happy. My business is very risky, but if you have a big heart, you can make it. Does that answer your question?" Andy asked Solomon.

"Yes, I like your answer. I'm also praying to be like you, and I admire your way of life. I will work very hard to become like you; that I can promise," Solomon said.

"OK, I don't want you guys to worry about money. Ebenezer, bring me that money on the table."

Ebenezer picked it up and handed it to Andy.

"Count it," Andy told him.

Ebenezer counted it silently.

"How much is there?"

"Thirty-nine thousand dollars."

"I made this money in just two hours from the time I dropped you off from the restaurant. This is one of the smallest amounts I've made in a long time. I don't want you guys to worry about money. All I want from you is your courage and respect for one another, and respect for the people you'll be working with.

"Now I want you guys to really listen to me, and if there's anything you don't understand, please ask me; I will be happy to answer your questions. I trust my brother, and I know he trusts you, and I'll base my judgment on that. Whatever we discuss here must stay here. Lots of people will be working with you. We promise to do all we can to protect their names."

He paused before continuing, and his voice grew more serious. "We steal containers and take them to our own location, then transfer the goods into our own containers, which go to our warehouse. We sell the goods to our customers. They buy them and ship them outside the country. We also get all the documentation for the types of goods they buy from us, and this enables them to take the goods out of the country without problem. Some also buy goods from us and sell them here.

"We have connections with various truck drivers, and when they are hauling containers, they call and tell us what they are carrying, what direction they will be heading, and where they will make their stops. Then I send my boys to steal the truck, and we do as I told you earlier.

"If we sell the products, we give them 20 percent. We never cheat, and we don't get them into trouble. This trust has been built over many years. It's solid now. About fifty to sixty truck drivers call me wherever they want to do business.

"This is how it works: When the trucks disappear, they wait a few minutes before notifying the police. By then our mission is complete, and the goods in the trucks are gone. Then the insurance companies deal with the loss.

"We get stuff like electronics, car parts, furniture, building materials—anything you can think of—and we have buyers lined up and waiting for our calls with the cash ready because our prices are cheap.

"In this business do not treat your coworkers as friends. They're your associates and nothing more. Keep everything you do to yourself and believe in yourself. Don't make friends, and if you do, don't tell them anything about your daily activities. You also have to be brave and strong. Expect jail because when you're living the fast life, jail is a harsh reality, but it makes you stronger and smarter.

"Even though I have been to jail seven times now, I still keep up my courage. Do you have any questions?" Andy asked.

Solomon spoke first. "Well, Andy, I think I understand everything, and I am looking forward to the job. I am not scared of jail at all, and I don't make friends."

"Yes, I agree with Solomon. I understand everything you said too," Ebenezer added.

"OK, I'll take you to my warehouse so you can meet my boys, and I will show you around. I'll teach you how I do my business. I'm happy that you guys understand me."

Solomon called his mother to let her know he had arrived safely and that he was fine.

"Please tell Mr. Carter thanks for the envelope. He gave me a money order for twenty-eight hundred dollars. I will cash it tomorrow when we go out in the morning. Tell him that I appreciate the letter he wrote expressing his concern. I understand, and I will stay in contact with him as I promised."

The next day Andy drove them to his warehouse, introduced them to his employees, and gave them a tour. Solomon's mouth dropped: The warehouse was enormous and crammed with all kinds of goods. He was instantly convinced that he was going to get rich.

That day they did a couple of business transactions and worked out a few deals with Andy before going home satisfied.

"Did you see how I treated you guys with that money I made? You saw how happy everybody was?" Andy asked.

"Yes, you're generous, and you give everyone what they deserve. I counted my share, and it came to $2, 253," Solomon said.

"I really like this boy. You answer with such knowledge and determination. It makes me confident that you'll become a great man quickly," Andy said. "Are you guys hungry? I'm not much of a cook, except for breakfast, so I'm taking you out to a restaurant." Andy said.

"If I was you, I'd probably do the same," replied Solomon.

Chapter 4

The next day Ebenezer and Solomon worked with Andy. He taught them and introduced them to more people. Andy worked with them until they were comfortable with everybody.

Within three months after their training, they both had saved sixty-six thousand dollars. On that monumental day, Andy turned his business over to them, including his apartment. He told them that he would be moving out within two weeks to his girlfriend's house, a woman who was also the mother of his son. He left Solomon and Ebenezer to work alone for those two weeks. They were sharing in all the money on a daily basis. After two weeks Andy called them into the living room.

"I'll be leaving you in charge of the business. I'm no longer a criminal. I'm going to quit the fast life now. I think I've made enough money to live the rest of my life comfortably. I'll be able to take care of my children and watch them grow happily. I want to give the two of you some last-minute advice before I leave. When you start working alone, you'll face a lot of temptation, and many other kinds of business deals will come your way.

"Many new clients will want to work for you, but heed my advice: You should not make any attempt to work with them. Don't be greedy. Always be happy with what you have. Work only with the people you've seen me working with and who know you through me. Please take my advice. My phone number is on the table. Don't bring anyone new to this house. With the money you make, you can take them to hotels or someplace else."

They both nodded in solemn agreement. He got up and shook their hands as they helped him take his bags out to his car. They packed everything in the trunk and in the backseat. When Andy was about to get into his car, he told them to remember to never drive directly to the warehouse but to take different routes to make sure nobody would figure out its location.

"You boys should not take any of these little precautions for granted; otherwise, you'll get into big trouble before you know it," he cautioned. That was the last time Solomon saw Andy.

Ebenezer and Solomon continued working together. The business was going well, and they were making good money for themselves. Solomon was playing it smart and giving the money that he made to his mother to keep in a safe place. He also bought a mechanic shop in

Queens that did bodywork and auto repairs for cover-up. After about three years, Solomon bought himself a three-bedroom apartment just four blocks away from Andy's apartment. He moved out, but he and Ebenezer continued to be best friends.

Solomon would take the weekends off to spend time with his mother in Brooklyn, who was getting quite concerned about the money she was keeping safe for him.

"Son, you and I have never really talked about what kind of business you're in to make all this money," she said. He lied to her that he was getting the money from his auto repair garage and that he cleaned offices at night.

"I work very hard," he told her. But his mother didn't believe him and told him that she didn't want to have anything more to do with his money; he should keep it himself. Solomon begged her, but she still refused to have anything to do with his money. Once he had all the cash, he didn't know quite what to do with it.

He thought about the man who was looking after his mother and his affairs, Mr. Carter. Solomon went to see him and was welcomed into the house. Solomon took Mr. Carter aside and told him everything about the money and that he needed his help.

"Are you sure if I keep this money for you that it will not bring me any problems?" Mr. Carter asked.

"You won't have any problems at all," Solomon promised him.

"Are you sure you have told me the truth about this? You know what will happen to me if something goes wrong, don't you?" Mr. Carter asked.

"Yes, sir, I told you the truth about my money. I couldn't tell my mother because it might break her heart. She doesn't want me to go in that direction and become a criminal. I've told you the truth because I know you're a man, and you can handle it. I don't want you to tell her anything I have told you," Solomon warned him. After a long talk, Mr. Carter agreed to help him keep his money without knowing the full amount.

"I'll bring it to you tonight because I don't want my mother to know where I am taking it."

While Solomon was at his mother's house that night, he got together with his old friend Jack Epstein who also was now living in New York. He went back home and took the money, which was stuffed into a big wooden box, to Mr. Carter's house.

Mr. Carter hastily took the money and said good-bye to Solomon, but Solomon asked him, "Where are you going to keep this money?"

"Don't worry, it's not your business," Mr. Carter said and turned to leave. Again Solomon said seriously, "Look, this is my money; I took great risks to get this money, which I've already told you about, and you're saying it's not my business to know where you're going to keep my money?"

"Correct," Mr. Carter said. "And if you don't trust me with your money, then take it." At that moment Solomon's face dropped with shame. He felt bad that he had doubted Mr. Carter.

"I will never doubt your trust again; please forgive me."

"It's all right. I forgive you because I know the strain you're under," replied Mr. Carter. Without a word Solomon walked away, got into his car, and drove to his mother's house. He spent the weekend with her before returning to business as usual on Monday.

One day one of his most trusted mechanics, Daniel Uvular, came to him with a business proposal. Towering over five-foot, Daniel was a chubby gentleman who had a positive attitude. Solomon welcomed the man into his office and sat down to listen to him.

"Sir," he said, "I want us to steal some luxury cars and bring them to our garage to remove the old registration numbers and resell them. We can buy these cars for peanuts and sell them for a lot of money."

"Do you know how stealing cars works?" Solomon asked Daniel.

"Oh sure, I know how to do it. I learned it from my former boss, and he was making all kinds of money doing it. I'm prepared to teach you everything you need to know about it because you're a good man. If you have any connections in foreign countries, you can ship them out there too," Daniel told him.

"That sounds like a good idea, but what I'm wondering about is how you'll get the cars," Solomon told him.

"That's the easy part. I know a lot of people that I trust who can steal cars for us. We would only pay three thousand dollars for a car that's worth about one hundred fifty thousand dollars. We could open a dealership where we buy cars from car auctions and sell them at our dealership. We can also sell cars that are stolen and nobody will ever know. Not even the other mechanics will know about it," Daniel replied.

"Like I said, it sounds like a good idea. I would be happy to work with you, but if you try to set me up, I will destroy you—including your family. Trust me." Solomon threatened with menace, and he got up to leave. He turned around and said, "Anytime you want us to start that business, just let me know, but remember that you should be honest with me."

Three weeks later Solomon had a talk with Daniel, who told him that he wanted to start the new operation the next day because he had already arranged for people to steal any type of car they wanted. Solomon told him that he wasn't ready for that yet.

"First of all I need to get a license from the government that will allow me to buy and sell used and new cars. I think it would be wise to start out that way," Solomon told him.

"That's a good idea. I'll wait for you," said Daniel.

Soon Solomon got the car dealership license from the government, and he was set. Everything was now up and running. The first month they sold almost all of the cars they had bought, so they went to the auction again and bought more cars. The garage and the dealership were doing very well. Solomon had money coming in from all over the place. He was getting rich and eventually struck up a friendship with some mafia bosses. With the money he was making, he rented a storage unit in Brooklyn far from his mother's neighborhood where he kept some furniture and some cash.

Chapter 5

Six months later the business was booming with people coming and going. Solomon called Daniel and told him that he was ready for him.

"Is there any special type of car you want?" Daniel asked.

"Yes. I would like a Porsche, Lexus, Mercedes-Benz, Cadillac, and Lincoln Navigator. Let me give you the money so you can pay the boys who are going to get them for you," Solomon said.

"No, sir, you keep the money. Give me a week, and you'll get everything you've asked for," Daniel told him.

Fourteen days later, as Solomon was returning from his container job, he went to the garage, and Daniel came over to him and said, "Follow me." They went to the back of the garage. Solomon couldn't believe his eyes. All the cars he had asked for were sitting there, brand new with plastic still on the seats.

"How much is all this going to cost?" Solomon asked.

"You only paid two thousand dollars for each of these cars. It'll take another five hundred to change the numbers and five hundred more to locate all the old numbers that the cars originally came with. For a job like this, we have to call in professionals because we can't afford to make any mistakes. Otherwise we'll not get too far," Daniel said.

Solomon looked at him and asked how many serial numbers each of the cars had and how they would all be found.

Daniel responded, "To be honest, I don't know how to do it, but I know professionals who can do it, and it's the only thing they are good at. They have a special machine that does the work for them, and they get them directly from the company. Don't be surprised to find out that your cars are double or boxed."

"What do you mean by double or boxed?" Solomon asked with concern.

Daniel stared at him and explained, "A double car is one that has been stolen, but instead of taking a different car, they go and buy the same type of car and use the serial number for both vehicles. Or you search the Internet for the same type of car located in another state and take the serial number from that car and put it on this car. That method only works if you want to ship it out of the country, but even with that, you'll have the same number for two identical cars in this country.

"If you want a box, you buy a car from the auction that has been in an accident and tell them you want to repair it and sell it. You bring that car to the garage and keep it. Then you send someone out to steal the same type of car. You call the professionals, who will take the number from the wrecked car and use their computers to locate all the numbers—including all the hidden numbers on that car—and you change them all to the wrecked car's number. Then you take the wrecked car, destroy it completely, and drop it off at a scrap yard for recycling.

"You make the stolen car legitimate by passing it off as the newly repaired wrecked car. You can sell the car for a higher price. Even the police won't see anything different, and you can even drive it yourself because it becomes risk free. You can do this to any car, but I prefer that you do it with only the most expensive cars on the market. That is what we call box. Hope you understand."

"Yes, I understand," said Solomon.

Solomon paid for the cars and did as Daniel instructed. He talked to some of his South American and Asian business associates to convince them to buy his cars and take them out of the country. They we excited about the business venture, thinking about the profit they would make, but they wanted to know more about the procedure.

Solomon went to Daniel, who clarified the process. "I know a fellow who can take the cars through customs for you, but the cars have to be packed in a container, and you should never use your own name when shipping them out. You'll have to find somebody in the country you're taking the cars to who can quickly and safely get them out of the foreign country's port. You don't have to worry about getting them out of here," Daniel told him.

Solomon was happy and passed the information on to his business associates. They were also pleased with the arrangement. He didn't tell Ebenezer about his new business.

One morning he told Ebenezer and his workers that he was going to Chicago and that he would be back in three days. Ebenezer was taken aback.

"Look, man, you know we have a big hit today, and you know that I need you on this. I can't do it by myself," complained Ebenezer.

"I know that we have a lot of work to do today, but I have already made plans to go," Solomon shot back. "I'm sorry, but I have to go."

"Well, if you insist, then I have nothing more to say. I'll do what I can alone. I hope you get back as soon as possible," Ebenezer said.

In Chicago, before arriving at his mother's relatives' place, he went to his grandparents' home. When they saw Solomon, they were very happy. His grandmother took the phone and called all her children, and a couple of hours later, the house was packed with the entire family. Everyone was eager to see Solomon.

"Where are you staying?" his grandparents asked him.

"I'm actually staying at a hotel. I just got here a few hours ago."

His family urged him to go back, pick up his bags from the hotel, and stay with them. His cousin gave him his car keys and a map of the city to help him get around. Solomon refused, but they kept at him, and he finally agreed when he saw how concerned they were about him.

"I'll drive you to your hotel," his cousin Jacob offered. Solomon retrieved his bags and went down to reception to check out. He went to stay with his family, and they wouldn't allow him to spend any of his money on food or clothes. They wanted to buy everything for him.

Solomon was touched by his family's concern. Even though two of his cousins and a couple of his uncles were facing problems with their mortgages, they still showered him with generosity. The next day he called a few real estate offices and went out with them to look for a nice house in a good neighborhood in West Town. He bought a house for $375,267 and furnished it. He gave his relatives the rest of the cash that he had with him and asked his Uncle James to follow him. They both flew back to New York, and Solomon gave him two hundred thousand dollars cash. He asked his uncle to take it back to Chicago and share it equally with the rest of the family, but that they should keep their mouths shut because he didn't want his mother to know about it. He didn't tell them anything about the house he had bought and furnished while he was there.

He took James back to the airport and didn't allow him to see where he lived or allow him to find out anything about his business. James didn't bother to ask him either. His sole concern was how to get the money back to Chicago safely.

The next day at work, it was business as usual. He was surprised with the progress Daniel had made while he was away. The storage area was filled with all kinds of cars worth ninety-five thousand dollars and up, and Daniel had already finished the entire job on them, so they were ready to be sold. Solomon was overjoyed.

Solomon went to work at the warehouse the following morning but later find out that Ebenezer was taking the day off to spend with his family. Solomon went to Ebenezer house and he welcomed him back and invited him into the living room. He brought out all the money they had made while Solomon was away in Chicago, but Solomon refused to take his share and told him to keep it for himself.

"Listen, Solomon, we're business partners. We are supposed to share any money that comes from the business. You're my best friend. Do you remember what your mother told us that morning before we came here? You're not only my best friend; you're my brother. Your mother told us to be fair with each other, and we would grow. So far that's what we've been doing, and we've never gotten into any trouble, and we should keep it that way. Now I'll keep your money for you until you come back," Ebenezer told him.

"Thank you, man," Solomon said and then left for work. When he finished work, he came directly to Ebenezer's house and picked up his cash. He went to use a pay phone in the street and called some of his customers about the cars for the next day, but to Solomon's surprise, all the cars had already been sold, and everyone was paid. Solomon smiled in quiet triumph. You could say it was a good day.

Chapter 6

One evening a man named Cooper, who used to steal cars for Daniel, boosted a nice BMW that was parked in a dealership. He was driving the car to Daniel because he had run out of money and needed to get some quick cash that night. Cooper had a friend who was desperate—this Irish gang didn't joke about the things they would do, and they would follow through on their threat to kill his little brother with no question.

Cooper and his friend were scared out of their minds and would have done anything to get the money they needed—even flouting the strict rules and regulations they all had to follow, despite knowing full well that any mistakes would have gotten every one of them thrown in jail.

While Cooper was driving the BMW, he didn't realize that two detectives, William Frowner and Newark David, were following him. But they didn't try to stop him; their plan was to follow him and see where he would take the car.

He drove to a familiar spot, parked the car on the street, and went into a bar. He sat at a window and watched to make sure that no one had followed him. He drank in contemplative silence and watched the BMW. The officers were parked on the other side of the street where they could see the car clearly. They waited patiently—eyes out for any movement around the car.

Cooper called Daniel at the shop from the bar, but nobody picked up. He sat there for another twenty minutes, watching the car before thinking to himself that maybe Daniel was just too busy to answer the phone. He decided he would take the car to the garage, which was nearby, because he knew Daniel would pay him.

Cooper left the bar and drove off. The detectives followed stealthily. At the garage he walked over to the receptionist and asked for Daniel, but he was told that Daniel was out. Cooper sat and waited while the detectives waited at the curb.

Two hours later, when Daniel returned to the garage, he saw the BMW and Cooper sitting in the waiting area. He told Cooper that he was not going to do any business that night, but he could leave the car in the garage and come back to get paid in the morning, but Cooper insisted that he really needed the money to save his friend's brother's life.

Daniel went outside to examine the car. Suddenly a car came screeching alongside. The doors flew open, and two detectives stepped out, shouting furiously, "Put your hands in the air!" They trained their guns menacingly at Daniel, who froze in shock. Cooper tried to run away, but one of the boys that worked in the garage caught him. Daniel came out of the car with his hands in the air.

"What are you doing in that car?" William Frowner demanded.

"I was just checking it out because he asked me to change the steering wheel, and I had to take a look at it," Daniel lied.

"Do you work here?" Newark David questioned.

"I work here as the manager of the garage."

Without saying anything further, they put handcuffs on Cooper and put him in the back of their car.

"Do you know this man?" Newark asked Daniel.

"No, I don't know him at all. I treat all my customers equally when they bring a car into my shop," Daniel told them.

"OK, just leave that car right there. Don't touch it. We will be back before midnight to pick it up. If you have any problems, you can call us. Take one of our cards," said Frowner.

"Thank you, sir," said Daniel, and the police left with Cooper in the backseat.

The two detectives drove him to a secure location and parked. They took him out of the car to speak with him.

"What do you do for a living?" Newark asked Cooper.

Cooper didn't even try to lie to them. "I steal cars and sell them for a living," he said.

"You'd better tell us everything you know, and it had better be the truth. If you lie to us, you'll go to jail for a very long time, but if you cooperate with us and tell us what we want to know, we will let you go. We will even let you have the BMW you just stole, and we will cover for you," William Frowner explained. "Do you understand?"

"Yes, I understand," said Cooper with a nod.

"Now tell us how you started doing this kind of work and why," Frowner asked.

"One day Daniel came to me in a bar and showed me a big roll of cash money, about seventy thousand dollars in hundred-dollar bills. I was broke, and when I saw all that money he had, I asked him if he was serious, and he told me that if I brought him cars, he would give me all that money. I stole the first car and brought it to him, and he paid me right away. That's how I got started."

"Who's this Daniel?" Newark asked.

"No, sir, I can't answer that question because I'd be destroying this business for a lot of other people like myself who are making a good living from this, and I can't do that," he told them.

"Look, young man, you have to tell us everything that we want to know; otherwise you'll go to jail for at least a few years," Newark David threatened.

Cooper looked at them confused and panicked, unsure of how to make his next move. He thought for an intense moment before deciding to tell them everything.

"Daniel is the man who was in the car when you guys arrived at the garage," he told them.

"Do you know what they do with all the cars that he buys from you and the others?" Newark asked.

"I don't know what he does with the cars because I've never asked him."

"Do you know the names of any other friends or people who sell him cars or sell to buyers like this Daniel fellow?" Newark asked.

"No. I only know of myself," he answered.

"How long have you known Daniel?" Frowner asked.

"About five years now," he told them. He sweated heavily as they stared at him with hardened gazes. "The first place he worked at closed down, and I didn't see him for almost a year—until he came looking for me. He asked me to start again, and that was the time he showed me that big roll of cash."

They wrote down all his personal information, told him that they weren't going to let him take the car, and any time they needed his help with the investigation, they would contact him. Cooper left hurriedly, euphoric over his sudden freedom, and faded into the night.

William and Newark went back to the station and checked the information they had received from Cooper and Daniel. They decided they would follow Daniel's every move. They instituted complete surveillance day and night.

Solomon and Daniel continued their business as usual, not realizing that the police were watching them and that Cooper had set them up. One month later, after one especially busy day, Solomon was tired. He had planned to go to the shop, but instead he went straight home to take a shower and get some rest. As soon as he arrived home, the phone rang. It was George, one of his customers who had bought his stolen cars.

"I want to talk to you if you have the time. I really need to see you. I have something important to tell you," George told him.

Solomon got up, dressed, and drove to the location suggested to meet the customer. When the two got there, they decided to leave the area and go somewhere else to talk.

Solomon asked, "What can I do for you? Why did you want to see me today so urgently?"

"I want to have some cars sent to Nepal. I have a lot of customers lined up who want them. Here is a list of the cars that I need. I'll pay you cash as usual, but I need them within ten days," George told him.

"I'll get them for you, but if I can't manage it, I'll let you know," Solomon told him.

"Look, Solomon, I trust you, and you're the only person I like to do business with. I'll call you in a couple of days' time to see how far you have been able to get with the cars." Solomon drove straight to the garage so that he could tell Daniel everything. They planned how they would do it.

"By tomorrow I'll tell you what we can and can't do about this. I'll go meet with a few of my boys and tell them what I need, and they'll tell me if they can do it all within the time frame," Daniel said.

Daniel then explained to Solomon what had happened earlier in the evening with Cooper and the two police officers. They knew that they would have to take their time and not do anything hastily because the cops would be watching them now.

"I want us to start taking the cars to our other used car parking lot at the back and do it from there. I think this place is only good for repairing and selling cars now—it's too dirty and marked for anything else. If we try to do anything more from here, we will be caught," Daniel told him.

"OK, anything you do—just make sure it's done right. When I see you tomorrow, we'll talk some more," Solomon said and left for home.

Chapter 7

Daniel worked quickly to finish things before the police could close in on them. The cars had already been sent out of the country, and when the police finally arrived, they found nothing.

The heat was on, but Daniel and Solomon were clever and careful. Andy's advice was never far from Solomon's mind. The following day Solomon came to see Daniel at the garage and told him that it was time to stop until they could be sure that things had cooled down.

"You're right. I really don't want to go to jail and lose everything," Daniel said in agreement, and he left to put his money in a safe place. Solomon decided to take the day off from working with Ebenezer.

Daniel was a rich man now, with more cash in his house than he could ever have dreamed of. But the weight of the dirty money was making him paranoid, so his wife took all the money to her mother's house and hid it for him. With the money safe, he went back to the shop, and business was going well. The dealership was packed with people coming and going, and a lot of them were buying cars.

Solomon put his complete trust in Daniel to run his business. He would stay away for weeks—even months. However, every day after work, Daniel would go to see him to report how much money they had made and to show him all the paperwork. He was kept informed daily about any activities that took place at his business.

Daniel started doing exactly what Solomon had told him not to do: he kept buying stolen cars and selling them. Business was booming as usual, and they were making more and more money, but he didn't let Solomon know what he was doing, and he didn't share any of the money he was making with Solomon. If Solomon knew, he would get rid of him, but Daniel's lust for the money was too powerful to resist.

Unfortunately what Daniel didn't know was that the police had plenty of information on the business because when they had arrested some of Daniel's men, they were trading information about Daniel. The police were preparing all their evidence against him. They were granted a search warrant from a judge.

When they burst into the dealership six months later, Daniel told them they needed a search warrant. Undeterred, they handed it to him. When they did their search of the dealership, down in the basement, they saw many expensive cars with people working on them, and they knew they had been stolen. They were caught red-handed, and Daniel was not able to escape the truth. Worse still, they also found about two hundred thousand dollars in cash in the safe of the dealership.

Everyone was arrested and taken to jail, and the police sealed all the doors of the dealership. They checked all of the cars and found that most of them had been stolen. They checked the ownership and found Solomon's name, but since he hadn't been seen coming to the shop, and he didn't appear to know what had been happening, he wasn't approached or arrested. Still the police chief ordered his men to start keeping close surveillance on him immediately.

The vise was tightening.

When Solomon didn't hear from Daniel one night, he didn't worry about it; however, the police had instituted surveillance on his house soon after arresting Daniel and had stayed there all night. The next day detectives Newark and William followed him to his warehouse. They sat and waited patiently for Solomon after documenting the name and location of his warehouse.

A short time later, they noticed a car leaving the warehouse with a truck following behind. The surveillance team quickly radioed in to have the truck followed. Solomon and Ebenezer were working in the warehouse on an order for their Indian customer. Hours later the truck returned and entered the warehouse. The police who had followed the truck reported information to the surveillance team, who wasted no time. They arrested eleven people, including Solomon and Ebenezer. The detective faces burst into wild smiles as they got their grip on Solomon and Ebenezer.

When they arrived at the police station, they were devastated to hear all the evidence against them. The police seized the computers that had prepared the original receipts for the cargo as well as cash and other items that could put them in jail for a long time. William Frowner and Newark David were excited that they had finally caught everyone who was responsible for many of their unsolved cases. They were kept in jail until all the evidence was put together.

One of the detectives questioned Daniel about his relationship with Solomon. Frowner stared at Daniel and said, "We meet again. The first time we met, you was the man; but now I am the man, and you will answer all of our questions correctly. Don't even try to play smart with us because it will just get you into more trouble.

"Who is Solomon, and how do you know him?" Newark asked.

"He is a good man. He taught me how to make money," Daniel answered.

"Make money in what sense?" William asked.

"He taught me about stealing cars. I was only working for him. Everything we did was his idea." He put all the blame on Solomon.

William and Newark prepared their case against Solomon and gave the information to the prosecutor, who used it to prepare a solid case against him. Solomon would be going to jail for a long time said Newark as William laughed.

Solomon called his mother, and she came to visit him in jail. He took his time and explained everything that had happened. Tearful but strong, she went back and told Mr. Carter, and they arranged to get Tom Romero as Solomon's lawyer. Tom Romero was a trusted man, and he had been with the Carter family for over ten years. He worked with Solomon to put together a case for his defense.

While they were waiting for the preliminary hearing, Newark and William went through all of Solomon's personal belongings in his house, and they found a card that had the address of the storage site on it. They took it to his friend Ebenezer, who wondered why Solomon would have a storage site card. After talking with Ebenezer, Newark and William took more officers with them and went to the storage unit to check on the contents of his unit. They obtained a spare set of keys and opened it up. They were shaken by what they saw. They found a lot of cash and other expensive items. They packed it all up and took it back to the police station. There was a mountain of evidence against Solomon, and they were set for the trial.

Meanwhile Mr. Carter was trying to help Solomon pay the heavy fees Tom Romero was demanding, but he promised that he would work very hard in Solomon's defense. Solomon's lawyer requested that he be allowed to see all the evidence the police had used to press the charges against him. It took some time, but he finally received the documents. He read everything, and when he was finished, he knew that Solomon didn't have a chance of winning his case; the evidence the police had was very strong.

Solomon's lawyer felt that his best option would be to plead guilty for a lesser sentence. Solomon had a good chance of getting it because he had no prior criminal record. In addition, the prosecutor was a good friend, and Tom thought that perhaps he could convince him to give Solomon a light prison sentence. The lawyer met with Solomon's mother and Mr. Carter to outline the whole situation and show them all the evidence the police had against Solomon. They looked for themselves and agreed that the lawyer knew what he was talking about. They told him to explain everything to Solomon and let him decide for himself.

The lawyer went to the jail and suggested that Solomon plead guilty in an attempt to get the lowest possible sentence; otherwise, with all of the evidence the police had, he could be looking at ten to fifteen years in jail. Tom also said that if Solomon thought he could win the case, perhaps they should go ahead with the trial. He made it clear to Solomon that he wasn't trying to deceive him, and Solomon could get another lawyer; the choice was his, but the lawyer was there to help him. Solomon asked if he could get a copy of all the evidence, and Tom arranged to have that done. Solomon read over all the documents and concluded that he would do exactly as his lawyer had suggested: he would plead guilty.

The next day he called Tom and told him his decision. But the looming doubt of how much time he would receive hung over Solomon's head and weighed on his heart. His lawyer told him he didn't know how long his sentence would be yet, but he would start the ball rolling and talk to the prosecutor to see what they could agree on. A few weeks later, Tom came to see Solomon and told him that an agreement had been made to sentence him to two years and five months if he would plead guilty to the charges.

***

Three months later Solomon's relatives showed up to support him at the preliminary hearing that morning. His lawyer called on him, and they talked about the case. The good news was that they had finally decided on a sentence of twenty-four months.

"I want you to trust me, and let's get this over with," Tom said. "The bad news is that you'll lose everything you've worked for—the garage, the money they found in the storage unit, and anything else they seized pertaining to your case. I know when you're out of prison, you'll be able to start a new life and maybe start a family someday."

Stoic and strong, Solomon listened carefully, taking it all in wordlessly.

They went into the court and sat down. Solomon, clad in prison coveralls entered the courtroom and sat down. He turned around and searched for his mother, to whom he waved and smiled. When Clare saw her son in that condition and thought about how his father died, she cried.

Chapter 8

After Solomon entered a guilty plea, he was given a twenty-four-month sentence from the judge and was led off by the prison guards to serve his sentence. Everything went just as his lawyer had told him.

They took Solomon to a small room and prepared all of his papers. Solomon had spent a long day waiting to be processed. They took his photograph and led him to the cell that he would be sharing with another inmate named Jimmy. Jimmy was a member of one of the Muslim gangs—the Muslim Brothers—and had a reputation for nastiness and ruthlessness. He was six feet tall and skinny, with a mustache around his mouth. He had a callous appearance.

There was no mattress on Solomon's bed, only bed sheets and a blanket scattered on top. There was a toothbrush, toothpaste, and some shampoo with a small comb. He sat down, ate his sandwich, and drank some water. He greeted Jimmy with a smile.

"Where can I get a mattress?" he asked Jimmy.

Jimmy roughly stared at him and asked, "Is this your first time in jail?"

Solomon looked at him for a moment, remembering what his old friend Jack had told him about prison, so he quickly said, "No, I've been in jail many times. This is my first light sentence."

"What are you in for?" he asked.

"It's a long story. I'll tell you some other time," Solomon said.

They sat there without talking for almost half an hour and then Solomon asked, "So what are the rules here in this jail?"

"You will find anything you want in here, even sex. If you want anything in this prison, come to me. I have been here far too long, and I basically know everything that goes on in here due to the strong connections I've built over the years. Besides this prison's rules are like every other prison you have been to."

During his first week in jail, Solomon got to know many inmates and made some friends. He dealt with everybody with respect, and he had a smiling face most of the time, so they started calling him the "happy guy."

After some time Mr. Carter came to visit him. When they saw each other, Mr. Carter was seized with emotion, and he broke down into tears.

"How are you doing? Have you been making some friends here?" he asked Solomon.

"I'm fine. I haven't had any problems so far because I stay in my own corner, and I don't take anything from anybody."

"Well, son, your lawyer told me that if you spend your time without problems, then you could get paroled to your house. Remember, I still have that little something you asked me to keep for you. It's in a safe place. Call me collect anytime you want. Try not to get into any trouble." After saying this, Mr. Carter got up and left.

***

A couple of months later, Solomon's mother and Mr. Carter came to visit him. Solomon received them happily. His mother said, "I have something very important to tell you. I'm moving back to Chicago. I've already put my house up for sale."

"But why do you want to do that, Mom?" Solomon asked.

"I'm now alone here. The rest of my family wants me to move back to Chicago. I will be happy with friends and family to look after me. Mr. Carter is the only person who sees me almost every day and talks to me for at least a few hours, but he is a busy man with his own family to take care of."

"I tried to talk to her, but your mother has made up her mind. Your mother needs to be around her people so she can forget about some of her problems. I support that," Mr. Carter said.

"Seeing as how you've already made up your mind, I just want to tell you that I already bought you a nice big house in Chicago. All of the documents are in your name. I furnished it too. I gave the keys to Grandma to keep for you, and it would be my greatest joy if you would take it," Solomon told her.

"What? You know that you're here in this jail because you made your money by stealing. I'm not a thief like you," she retorted. "What makes you think that I'll take anything from you that you bought with dirty money? You can keep it for yourself, so that the day you leave this jail, you'll have a place to stay."

Solomon looked his mother and said, "Mom, if you don't take this house, I will kill myself in this jail. Don't you know that you're the only person who can make me happy? I want to take good care of you. I want to do for you what I promised."

"All your promises and your big thinking and your big mouth don't move me at all. I still love you as my son, and nothing will ever change that, but I want you to start doing things right. Think about your future from now on. I know that if you had been going to school as you promised your father before he died, you would be finished with your studies by now, and that promise would be fulfilled."

"Mom, if you love me and you want me to live for you, then you had better take what I bought for you. I'm sure you know all of the problems

I went through just to get you that house." "You can't scare me at all," she responded firmly. "So don't sit here and threaten me."

Mr. Carter looked at Solomon, leaned back, and said to Clare, "I think this boy is serious about what he is saying, and I want you to take him seriously."

Clare asked, "Why did you give the house keys to my mother?"

"She was the only person I trusted at the time, and I knew she would help me keep everything a secret. She'll give you the keys, and you'll love the house. It's in a rich neighborhood, and it's even bigger than the house you're living in now. I furnished it just the way you would want it."

"How would you know how I like my house to look?" she asked.

"I'm your son. I've been living with you from the day you gave birth to me. I have watched you carefully to see what you love and don't love. You'll be surprised that Grandma and Grandpa also put some things in the house that they said you loved when you were growing up," Solomon said.

"Well, I'll see it when I go there the day after tomorrow. If you call the house and I don't answer, then you can call your grandparents collect, and we will accept your call and speak to you," she said.

"Oh no, Mom, I don't want any of them to know that I am in jail. I want you to promise me that you'll not tell any of them about it," he said.

"I already told them all about it. I'm sorry," she said.

"Oh my God! I knew it," Solomon said and put his hands on top of his head. His eyes reddened.

"I'm only playing with you," she smiled gently. "I didn't tell them about your problems. I told them that you have traveled to the Caribbean on vacation. If there's ever a need for me to tell them, I will because I won't lie to any of them again; if they found out that I did lie, they would lose confidence in me," she said.

Mr. Carter spoke. "I think it's late. Don't make any unnecessary friends. Remember that if you do well and get yourself a job or go to school, you'll have an easier time getting your parole sooner." They shook hands and kissed him on the forehead. She told him to take good care of himself. The guards escorted them out while Solomon was taken back to his jail cell.

Chapter 9

Solomon's mother sold her house and moved to Chicago. She was living there now but sent him letters and postcards every week and came to visit him once a month.

Solomon's fate took a fortunate turn when he was granted parole after a year. However, one of his conditions was that he couldn't leave New York until his sentence was over. He accepted this condition and promised to obey all of them. Solomon was released, and Mr. Carter brought him to his house. Solomon stayed there for two weeks until he found a place to live in Brooklyn.

A week later he found a job through a job placement agency, which assigned him to a warehouse where he was responsible for loading and unloading trucks that brought in supplies. He worked like a robot that first day; after work he went home exhausted, and his body was sore. He stood in a hot shower and didn't really want to come out for the longest time. He decided to quit that job.

The next morning he got up and thought about his bail conditions. He needed to find another job, but he had no work experience or qualifications to speak of, and he didn't want to go back to jail. He decided he would go back to the warehouse job. It was full time and hard work, so he would make money but be too tired to spend it. He got plenty of exercise at work, so he didn't need to go to a gym.

Other interests filled the void in his new life. He developed a great passion for women and became a complete womanizer. If he could, he would have sex with every woman he saw. One day he went to a nightclub to have some fun and try to pick up a girl. He was really enjoying himself that night. He asked a girl to dance, and they started having fun. They began kissing, and Solomon was sure that they would go back to his place that night. He bought her drinks, and as they danced, their mutual attraction was obvious and growing, but he neglected to ask her if she had come alone. A short time later, her boyfriend returned to the club, and his friend told him what was happening between Solomon and his girlfriend.

Furious, the boyfriend charged up to Solomon and pointed a gun at him. "Do what I say, or I'll shoot you," the boyfriend growled. "I won't think twice to shoot you now. I'm high as hell, fool!"

"Let's go outside through that door right in front of you," he told Solomon.

Solomon complied with everything he said. They went outside and stood in the street behind the club.

"Now you tell me, why were you all over my girl tonight?" he asked Solomon roughly.

"What girl are you talking about?" Solomon shot back.

"The girl you were dancing with and kissing in the club tonight. She is my girlfriend. Let me tell you something: The next time I see you hanging around my girl, I'll kill you. I'll shoot you in the head, and I can do it. I'm good at it, and if I were you, I wouldn't go back into the club unless you want to get yourself killed."

He put the gun back in his pocket and angrily walked away. Solomon stood there, thinking about his brush with death. He walked down the street, bought a bottle of water, and drank it in silence. He decided to take the bus home. He thanked God for keeping him safe, and he promised not to go back there anymore. He continued to work and stayed in contact with his mother, Mr. Carter, and his parole officer.

***

Across the street from where Solomon was living, there was a Catholic girls-only high school. Every morning and evening, he admired all the beautiful girls passing by. Sometimes they talked to him and asked how he was feeling. He was a handsome young man, and women were attracted to him. One of the girls, Teresa, seemed very interested and wanted to know more about Solomon. That was the origin of their friendship. Every day after school, they spent some time together at Solomon's place, and after some time Solomon ended up falling in love with her and wanted to marry her. She talked about taking Solomon home to meet her parents, so they set up a time and she gave him the address.

Solomon got all dressed up. He took a bus close to her house and then took a taxi the rest of the way. When he arrived he rang the doorbell, and Teresa's father answered the door.

"What do you want?" he asked.

"I'm your daughter Teresa's friend, and she invited me here today," Solomon told him.

He looked Solomon up and down and then yelled, "Teresa, somebody by the name of Solomon is here to see you!"

Teresa quickly came to the door. "Dad, this is Solomon. I told you about him some time ago. He is my boyfriend."

Without saying anything to Solomon, he turned and went back into the house, leaving them alone at the door.

"Come on inside, Solomon. Don't mind my dad. Sometimes he behaves like that," Teresa said. Solomon went into the house. He was invited to stay for dinner with them, and while they were sitting at the table, Teresa told her parents that she had something to tell them. They all stopped eating and turned to listen to her. She looked at them, looked at Solomon, and said, "Solomon and I are getting engaged next week." Her parents were totally shaken at this news.

"Can I speak to you for a minute, Solomon?" Teresa's father asked solemnly.

Solomon got up and followed him outside to the yard. "Wait for me here; I'll be right back." Solomon stood there waiting for him. When Teresa's father came back out, he pointed a gun directly at Solomon and told him to sit down on the ground. He said it very seriously. Solomon thought, *What bad luck this is*, but sat down on the ground.

"My daughter is just a little girl, and we want her to go to school and get an education. We don't want her going out with some psycho we don't like at all. I could kill you right now and tell the police that you attacked me in my own home. I could tell them that I had no choice but to shoot you. They will believe me, and you'll go to hell. Let me warn you, young man, if I ever see you around my daughter again, or if you even speak to her, I swear to God I'll kill you." As he spat out his last words, he hit Solomon in the stomach with the butt of the gun.

Solomon crumpled to the ground. He then got up and ran out of the yard in pain, thinking that he only had two more months of parole left; he didn't want to end up going back to jail.

When he got home, he cried from the pain he felt in his stomach and the trauma of the whole experience. He didn't go to work the next day. He stayed home and took some painkillers. He stayed in his house until he felt better.

Teresa came to apologize for what her father had done to him, but he told her that he would not see her again and that their relationship was over. He told her not to even speak his name again. That touched off a bitter, heated argument, but from that day on, Solomon was careful in picking his women. He preferred paying prostitutes to have sex; he thought it was safer than having a girlfriend.

He stuck close to his own home until his parole was finally over about two months later.

One sunny, bright day, Solomon decided to take advantage of the weather by taking a walk around the neighborhood to sort out his thoughts. While walking down his street and enjoying the sun, a green Cadillac Catera stopped beside him. At the wheel was a girl who had been watching him and wanted to get to know him.

"Excuse me, sir, do you need a ride? I can see that we're going in the same direction."

Solomon stopped and looked at the beautiful, mysterious woman sitting behind the wheel.

"Thank you, but I was just going for a walk. That is kind of you, but I'm fine," Solomon said.

"I just want to talk to you, that's all," the young woman insisted.

Unable to resist her beauty, Solomon got into the car. He stretched his hand out to shake her hand and introduced himself.

"My name is Mary. It's nice to meet you. I know Brooklyn very well. So are you married, or do you have a girlfriend or someone you're involved with?" she asked.

"No, not right now, but why do you ask?"

"Just curious," she replied. "So what are you doing this weekend?"

"I have no idea. Usually I rent movies, buy food, and stay home," Solomon told her.

"Are you telling me that you don't have any friends at all?" she asked.

"I have no friends, and I hate making new friends. I'm not very lucky with them. I try to stay as far away as possible from people," Solomon said.

"That sounds strange. You're just like me. I don't have any friends either. Most of the friends that come around are jealous of me. My parents tried to tell me that I wasn't very lucky in making friends, and when I really thought about it, I decided to cut them all off," she said.

"Why did you ask me about my plans for the weekend?" Solomon asked.

"Well, I have something in mind. Why don't you and I see each other and spend some time at your place? I'll come and visit you on Sunday," she said.

"Does that mean you're asking me for a date? I've never had a woman ask me for a date, but you know what, I would be happy to meet with you. It would be my pleasure," he told her with a smile.

Chapter 10

After dinner that night, he watched television for a while before going to bed. Solomon went to work for the rest of the week, and on Saturday he rented some newly released movies and brought them home. He cooked some chicken breasts and brought the phone close to him while he watched the movies and waited for his new friend, Mary, to call. Finally toward evening, Mary called. They talked for an hour and set a time for three o'clock on Sunday. Solomon was eagerly looking forward to it.

The next day he went to the supermarket to buy food and drinks. He cleaned the entire house and sprayed it with air freshener. He put a bottle of wine in the fridge and cooked a nice sticky lemon chicken and also prepared some garlic toast for the meal. He also picked up some romantic movies they could watch together.

At two o'clock he went for his shower and took his time getting dressed in his dinner suit. He sampled the food he had cooked to make sure it tasted just right, but he didn't want to eat too much before Mary came over. Then he sat down to watch television while he waited for his date to arrive.

Shortly thereafter a knock sounded at the door.

"I'm happy to see you. Wow! Look at you. You're so beautiful," Solomon told her.

Mary smiled and thanked him. He held her hand and brought her into the living room.

"Your house is beautiful and so clean. Are you normally a clean person, or did you clean just because of me?" she asked.

"My dear, I'm a very clean person. I try to keep the house tidy every day."

"That's good. I love clean people. After five years I'm finally entering a man's house," she said and sat down. Solomon's living room had a gray sofa, a white rug on a pale wooden floor, and a large window.

"Would you like something to drink?" he asked.

"Oh yes. Could I have a glass of water, please?" she replied.

"I have red wine if you prefer. I got it especially for you, but I don't know if you'll like it," he said.

"Well, I'll take some red wine then."

Solomon quickly poured the wine into two glasses. They toasted each other and took a sip.

Then Solomon prepared and served the dinner. After she sat down, he went to the other end of the table, facing her. "I hope you don't mind that everything here is very small, but this is how it was actually built. I want you to feel free and treat this house like your own. I hope you enjoy the food that I prepared just for you."

They ate, and when they had finished, they talked.

"So do you have any brothers and sisters?" she asked Solomon.

"No, I'm the only one."

"What a coincidence. I'm an only child too," she said. "So what do you do for a living?"

"I do shipping and handling—sometimes loading. It's very hard work, trust me," he told her.

"What company do you work for?" she asked.

"Right now, I'm working in a warehouse that belongs to Walmart," he answered. The job is difficult, so when I come home at the end of the day, I usually go straight to sleep because I am so tired. I am looking for a much easier job, but they are difficult to find. What do you do for a living?" Solomon asked Mary.

"I just completed my MBA, and I specialize in banking and finance. I'm supposed to get a job working for my parents, but I think I'll look for a job somewhere else because their business is not doing too well," she said.

As Solomon and Mary talked, they discovered a love blossoming between them.

"Can I kiss you?" she asked.

"Sure," he said. They kissed until she felt horny and wanted to have sex. While she was trying to take off Solomon's shirt, he backed away from her, saying they should get to know each other better before they got into anything like that. She looked at Solomon, and tears filled her eyes. Solomon held her in his arms and tried to comfort her.

"There are better days ahead of us. We have so many things to enjoy in our future together. I love you, I really do, and I don't want to lose you. That's why I think we should take our time," Solomon said.

"You're right. I'm sorry. I haven't slept with a man for a long time, so I got carried away when you kissed me," she said.

They stayed together for four hours until she told him that she had better be going home. He escorted her to her car, and she drove off. Solomon was pleased with himself for not having sex with her.

As time went by, they saw more of each other and talked on the phone. Two months later Solomon asked if he could visit her at her house. She didn't want to take him to her house because she didn't want him to see how wealthy she was, so she quickly rented a small one-bedroom apartment in a very old building in the Bronx to pass off as her home. Once it was furnished, she brought him there, and they stayed for most of the night. Solomon left at three o'clock in the morning so he could get to work on time later that morning.

After a year had passed, they were still seeing each other every weekend. Mary had complete confidence that Solomon was the man for her. What she didn't know was that Solomon had been to prison, he used to have sex with prostitutes every night, and he had been the leader of a criminal organization.

One day, as they were riding in her car, Mary went in a direction they had never been before. They drove to a big house where well-dressed servants welcomed her home. She parked the car, and one of the servants opened the door for her and helped Mary out of the car.

"What's going on here? Why are we here?" Solomon asked curiously.

"This is where I live. I live with my parents, and they are waiting for us." She took his hand as they walked into the house.

"But you didn't tell me that you were rich! You've never talked about it the whole time we've been together," Solomon said.

"Now you know. Come on; let's go in before it gets late."

"I don't think this should go on any further. I've told you everything about myself from the beginning, and all you've done is lie to me. I don't think that's right," he said. "I'm sorry, but I think it's time for you to find a new man." He left angrily and walked to the main road to catch a taxi home.

Mary was devastated, but she didn't try to stop him from leaving. She thought that if she gave him some time, he would calm down.

She didn't call Solomon for three weeks. His love for Mary was deep and real, not because of what she had but for who she was. He couldn't sleep or eat. The two weeks felt like two years. He didn't want to call her because Mr. Carter had suggested that he wait until she called him first.

One month later, on a Saturday afternoon, Mary dressed up and, with her manservant, knocked on Solomon's door. Solomon had stayed at home that day and was alone, watching a movie. Earlier that day he had hired a prostitute, but she had left two hours before, and he had cleaned his entire house. When he opened the door, he could hardly believe his eyes.

"You look great! I can't believe you came back. After all this time, you finally came to see me," Solomon said with a smile. He invited them inside.

"How do you know that I came to see you?" she asked him.

"Because you're standing here," he answered. "Who's this guy?"

"He's my bodyguard. I brought him to watch my back. This way I'm prepared for anything," she said.

"I really did miss you. I'm happy to see you again. Come in." Solomon welcomed her into his house for the second time. She asked her bodyguard to wait for her in the car.

"I think you told me the truth about yourself, and I did not. I'm sorry, but I've had problems in the past with other boyfriends. When they saw everything that I had, they took advantage of me. They used me to get things they wanted, but they were really in love with other women. It hurt me so much that I never wanted to get involved with another man until I met you. I'm looking for true love; that's why I didn't tell you about myself. I knew it was wrong that I kept the truth from you, and that is why I am here to apologize," she said.

"You don't have to apologize to me anymore. I'll try to make you happy, and I will do everything in my power to convince you that I love you. I have found you to be a lovely, kind, and respectful woman, and I want you to be a part of my life," Solomon told her.

"I didn't realize what a lovely human being you are. I missed you too. I'll also do everything in my power to keep you happy."

Solomon looked at her and paused for a moment. "You really played me. I really believed that you were the person you said you were. I just hope and pray that you never lie to me again. I love you just the way you are. I want you to be the mother of my children," Solomon told her.

Mary was overjoyed at his words. She hugged him and said, "If you love me, then we will have to go and see my parents."

"When do you want us to go?" he asked.

"Right now," she replied.

Solomon quickly got dressed in black jeans and a clean white shirt. He followed Mary to her car and drove to her place.

Chapter 11

At Mary's house Solomon sat comfortably on the brown leather sofa; Mary's parents sat close by him. Mary father was the owner of a small oil refinery in Houston, but the head office was in New York. Mary's mother asked about Solomon's parents as well as his family life, and he quietly explained everything to them about his life and his parents, but he left out the part about his time in prison. Solomon told her what he did and made her believe that he was working hard to have a great future, which amazed Mary's mother. They sat and talked for a long time. Mary was surprised that Solomon seemed to make a good impression on her mother.

"You know, son, when I met my husband, he had the same goals about who he wanted to be," Mary's mother said. "He always told me to think big. You're the very first young man that Mary has ever brought to this house and introduced us to. Maybe that's why I'm so comfortable with you. I trust Mary's judgment, and it's a pleasure having you in our home."

"Thank you very much. I'm happy that you accept me into your family. I'll do my best to treat Mary right and make her happy. She is the only woman in the world that I have ever loved, and I want to spend my life with her."

"That's wonderful," said Mary's mother. She had long hoped to see her little girl happy; as she looked in her daughter's eyes, she was relieved that Solomon had come into Mary's life and loved her truly.

Two months later, with the money he had saved, Solomon bought a beautiful ring for Mary. It cost him all of his money, and he didn't even have a car to drive. Mary came to visit him that day. He had already ordered pizza, cleaned the house, and adorned the table with candles. He had also sprinkled red roses all over the floor in the dining room and living room, allowing their pleasant scent to fill the house.

"The house smells really nice and sweet. What have you been doing here?" Mary said as she walked in. When she saw the red roses scattered all around, she picked one up and smelled it. "What's with the roses all over the floor? What's going on here?" she asked.

Solomon stood there not saying anything. Mary went into the living room and sat down. Solomon had even strewn roses on the couch. Solomon went over to her, kissed her, and asked her to come with him to the kitchen. She followed him and saw the candlelight on the table. She was sure that Solomon was going to ask for sex that night.

She sat down at the table. Solomon brought the food and put it on the table. They ate and drank some red wine. The food was delicious, the drinks were good, and the conversation was scintillating. Mary was having one of the best days of her life with a man she loved very much.

A little while later, while they were talking, Solomon looked at her and said, "You know that I love you. You're the woman I want to spend my life with. You mean so much to me, and I couldn't live my life without you." With a smile, he knelt down in front of her and took out the ring. "Will you marry me?"

Mary couldn't believe what she was hearing. She had wanted this for a long time. With tears of joy running down her face, she knelt down, kissed him, and answered, "Yes, I do want to marry you," and then she hugged him.

Solomon put the ring on her finger. Full of joy, Mary grabbed the phone and called her mother. Both parents were so happy for their little girl that they started singing and dancing.

That night Mary slept over at Solomon's house. It was the first time they had sex, and it was the first time they had shared a bed and slept together in the same house. The sex was so good that she could still feel Solomon's warm body the next morning. She felt a deep connection to Solomon that increased her affection for him even more.

After a six-month engagement, they were still not living together. One night after dinner, they discussed their wedding plans. Solomon didn't want a big wedding, but Mary eventually persuaded him.

The invitations were prepared and sent out to everyone. Mary's parents sprang into action to make their daughter's wedding day one to remember. They didn't care how much money they spent.

The wedding was held in the Catholic Church that Mary and her parents had attended for years. There were two hundred people in attendance with a TV crew. It was so crowded that people were standing outside. Everyone was dressed in his or her best clothes, and everything went off without a problem.

The wedding reception was held in a large convention hall. All the guests enjoyed themselves the entire day and night, and Solomon and Mary were very happy. Solomon's mother felt it was the best thing that had ever happened in his life. She shed many tears of happiness for her little boy. Mr. Carter and his family were also very happy for Solomon. Everyone was in good spirits and content.

For their honeymoon Mary and Solomon spent a week in Stockholm, Sweden. While they were there, Solomon didn't visit the place where his great-grandparent lived because they were on vacation in Chicago.

Once the newlyweds had returned, they found that Mary's parents had purchased a new house for them and had furnished it while they were away.

The house was not too far from their house. They were also presented with a key to their new Lincoln Navigator, which they drove from the airport to their new house. The house was big and beautiful and full of everything one could imagine or desire, including a swimming pool and a tennis court. They fell in love with it as soon as they saw it. When they entered the garage, there was a brand-new Toyota Corolla waiting for them.

Mary's parents had also deposited money into a bank account so they could purchase anything else they might need for their new house. They were all set to start their new life.

The next day Mary spoke to Solomon after she'd had a long talk with her parents. They went into Mary's mother's office. Solomon looked into her eyes and was anxious to hear what she had to say.

"I talked to my parents, and as you know, they are getting older. They want to retire and go on a cruise, so they can spend some time together. They trust me, and they know that with my education I have the ability to take over their business, which is just what they want me to do. They want you to help me run the business," she told him.

Solomon protested.

"Solomon, you're now my husband. We are one flesh in the eyes of God. This is our business, and thousands of people work for us. You'll be your own boss, and you'll have your own office with a secretary who will be ready to do as you ask."

"You're right. I should be by your side," Solomon said.

"Let's go so I can show you the company offices." They went to say good-bye to Mary's parents and then drove to the office.

Mary showed him all around and introduced him to the managers. She showed him where his office would be and said he could redecorate it or change anything he wanted, and the company would pay for it. Solomon was happy with the idea that he was now in charge of a big oil company with thousands of people to control. He felt he would be happy there.

Two weeks later he moved all his stuff from his old house into their new house. He called on the old couple who had allowed him to stay in their house rent-free and thanked them profusely. He also handed them some money to thank them for their kindness.

When the redecorating of his office was completed, Solomon started work. Mary was in an office on the sixth floor, and Solomon was on the first floor. After a few months of marriage, Solomon started to feel a little differently about their relationship. They were spending too much time together between work and home. Mary wanted to go everywhere with him and do whatever he wanted to do. Even while they were at the office, she would call him every half hour just to talk to him.

Moreover she became jealous and would get mad if she saw Solomon talking with another woman at a party or at the mall. It got to be a little too much for him, and he started having problems sleeping. He was afraid to approach her about it because he thought that she might kill him.

In need of a break, Solomon went to Chicago for a few days. Mary had called Solomon at his office, and the secretary told her exactly what Solomon had asked her to say. He told her that he would be late for work. Mary kept on calling, but there was no word from Solomon. Mary carried on with her duties. When she finally went home, she called for Solomon, but he wasn't around. There were no messages on the machine, so she sat and waited for him to call. She waited the whole night, but there was still no word or sign of Solomon.

The following day Mary went to her doctor's appointment and found out that she was three months pregnant. When she got home, she called the police to report that her husband was missing.

Mary eventually learned that Solomon had taken a flight to Chicago the day before. When she returned home, she thought that she should go to Chicago and find Solomon. She believed it would be easy for her to find the house where Solomon's mother lived.

Mary felt very sad. She was three months pregnant, and she didn't want to have a baby without a father. Mary made up her mind that if she didn't find Solomon or any of his relatives within the next month, she would have an abortion.

Mary couldn't sleep that night, and it was one of the longest nights she had ever had. The next morning she booked a flight to Chicago. On arrival she went to a taxi stand and took out Clare's address. The cab driver looked at it and told her he had a good idea of where to go.

Chapter 12

Meanwhile Solomon was on a binge. He had spent some time hanging out with his friends, drinking, having sex with prostitutes, and generally having fun. That day he didn't go out but was in his room staring at a picture of his wife and thinking about her. He was sad as he wondered how his lovely wife was doing. He was actually thinking of returning to her.

The taxi driver finally found the address Mary was searching for. She paid him and told him to keep the change. She picked up her bag and walked up to the house. It was a big, beautiful house. Solomon's mother was sitting in the living room, reading a book and waiting for Solomon to come out of his room. She heard the knock at the door, and although she wasn't expecting anyone other than Mr. Carter later that day, she thought one of her family members who lived in the neighborhood had decided to stop by. She opened the door and to her surprise saw Mary standing at the door

"Come in, dear," Clare said. "Are you all right?"

"No, I'm not all right," Mary replied.

"What happened, my dear?" Clare asked.

"Have you seen Solomon lately?" Mary demanded.

"Yes, he's in his room. He told me you couldn't come with him because you were busy with your job. I believed what he told me even though it was hard to do so," Clare said.

Mary asked, "Which way is his room?"

"Come, I'll show you."

Mary followed Clare to Solomon's room.

Mary walked straight to the door and knocked. She was nervous.

"Who is it?" Solomon asked.

Mary didn't say anything.

"Come inside," Solomon said in a tone that told Mary he was in some kind of distress.

Mary opened the door slowly and stood there. Solomon was sitting on his bed holding Mary's picture. He didn't even turn around to see who was at the door.

"It's me," Mary said.

Solomon quickly turned when he heard her voice. He threw himself at her feet, crying.

"I am so sorry. I don't know what came over me. I was confused and didn't think you were really in love with me. Please don't leave me! I'm so sorry. I need your forgiveness; please forgive me!"

Mary couldn't hold her anger anymore, and she started to cry.

While this was all going on, Mr. Carter arrived at the house.

Solomon's mother opened the door for him, and the two of them went to see what was happening in Solomon's room. When his mother entered the room and saw them holding each other and crying, she started to cry too.

Mary asked Solomon, "What happened? What did I do that made you run away from me? I want you to be honest with me. I know you'll not lie in front of your mother and Mr. Carter."

"You know that I love you, dear, but I didn't like some of the things you were doing, and I was afraid to say anything to you. It was getting to be so much for me that I couldn't deal with it anymore. I felt I had to run away from you," Solomon told her.

"But, dear, you're my husband, and we are one now. If you thought I was hurting you in any way, you could have told me. We are supposed to let each other know about what we like and don't like about each other's behavior. I didn't realize that I was hurting you. I love you, and I want to be with you as much as I can. You are the only man for me, and I don't want to lose you over something stupid like this. Why would you be scared of me? What evil have I ever done to you?" Mary said.

Solomon looked so forlorn that his mother and Mr. Carter decided to help him and talk to his wife. The problems were finally settled, and Mary promised to give Solomon whatever space he needed and to respect his privacy.

Mary stayed at Clare's house for another two days with Solomon, and everyone was happy to hear the good news that Mary was expecting a baby. Clare warned Solomon to be kind to his wife, and during the time they spent in the house in Chicago, she found Mary to be a very likable woman. She was smart, intelligent, and hardworking—Clare just loved her. She was happy that Solomon had met such a nice woman who knew how to treat people kindly and with respect.

"Do you know how many men are looking for such a woman? We are not looking at what she has but who she is on the inside, and I tell you, boy, she's a godsend," Clare told her son.

"Mama, I want to thank you for being such a strong mother. You never gave up hope for me. You always believed in me. Today I am who I am because of your determination as a mother. You're my best friend. There was a time in my life when I wanted to walk away from the things you believed that I could do. I thought they were too hard for me and were taking too much of my time, but you were always by my side, telling me to be patient and have faith in myself. You knew me better than I knew myself, and you always knew what was best for me.

"Today, when I look back at my life, I realize how stupid I was back then. If I could turn back time, I would do everything you wanted me to do with my life. I'm a man now with a wife to take care of, and no words can express how thankful I am for you. I love you so much. I will appreciate your motherly love for the rest of my life. Thank you, Mom," Solomon finished.

Filled with happiness and joy, Clare started crying. She looked in Solomon's eyes and could see his utter sincerity. A wave of pride surged through her.

"I'm very proud of you, and I love you too, Solomon. Take good care of your wife."

***

When Mary and Solomon arrived in New York, they resumed the happiness they were accustomed to, but Mary never told her parents that Solomon had run away because she was too ashamed of that whole experience to talk about it.

She also had a secret lover with whom she was sexually active with. He happened to be Deon Clautier, her personal assistant. He was a muscular, handsome, five-foot-seven gentleman with a breathtaking smile. He had black hair, a mustache, and brown eyes. He was a French Canadian from Montreal, Quebec.

A few months later, Mary gave birth to a baby boy whom she named Bobby. He was a happy little boy who always had a smile on his face.

Solomon's mother came to New York and took care of the baby for almost a year before returning to Chicago. Three years later another child, a girl, was born, whom they called Barbara.

When Barbara was six and Bobby was nine, Solomon started having a secret lover from his workplace, and they fell in love. Her name was Julianne Gorier, and they pretended that neither one noticed the other in the office. Seven months later she came to Solomon and told him that she was pregnant. He was surprised, and he begged her to have an abortion. This hurt and angered her because she thought Solomon truly loved her and would never ask such a thing of her. She threatened to tell Mary about her pregnancy. Solomon brushed it off as an empty threat, but Julianne followed through.

When Mary heard about it, she was furious. She confronted Solomon, who didn't deny it. She couldn't accept it and told him to leave the house. She said she didn't want to see him or have him around their children anymore.

Solomon realized the danger around him, and in order to keep things calm, he checked into a hotel where he lived for nine days until he found himself a one-bedroom apartment in a beautiful building.

After Solomon moved into the apartment, he tried to keep in contact with his children, but Mary refused to let him see them. His mother tried to intervene for the sake of her grandchildren, but that failed. He was not allowed to go to the house or see his kids until the divorce was finalized and decisions had been made concerning who would have custody of the children.

He looked for a new apartment in a much more distant neighborhood. Solomon was now in need of work, so he contacted an old friend named Mike; but after having a long discussion with him, Solomon's worries deepened. He realized that Mike's business wasn't the right fit for him. He was a notorious gang leader, and Solomon didn't want to be involved in or have anything to do with criminal activities. He only wanted to work legitimately.

As for Ebenezer, he had gone right back to working for his brother, Andy, after his prison sentence. He stood firm on his commitment to his brother's business but refused to have anything to do with Solomon.

Chapter 13

Meanwhile Solomon had a chance encounter with two taxi drivers at a bar. They gave him their cards and told him they had a job for him.

After his morning shower, Solomon called one of the taxi drivers, a man named Smith. He answered the phone and gave him directions to their office. Solomon drove there. When he entered, he saw Matthew and Smith grinning at him.

"We were waiting for you," Smith said.

"I know."

"Can we see your identification that I asked you to bring?"

Solomon handed his driver's license to Smith.

They used his information to fill out an application, and then they asked him to read and sign several documents. They gave him a list of their rules and regulations, as well as his rights as a driver. Solomon easily passed the driver training exams. Smith and

Matthew took him to their taxi stand and showed him where he would start.

The first day on the job was a tough one for Solomon, but he decided to see the bright side of the job and enjoy it. Solomon's bosses were pleased with his performance. He came to love his job and never missed a day of work.

A year later Solomon thought he knew everything about his job, so he decided to buy his own taxi and apply for a license from the government to run his own service. He turned to the man who had been serving as his father figure for help. When Mr. Carter saw how serious Solomon was about what he wanted to do, he decided to lend him fifty thousand dollars. As he was writing the check, Mr. Carter reminded Solomon that some time ago, before Solomon went to jail, Solomon had given Mr. Carter some money in a wooden box to hold in safekeeping for him.

"Oh yes, I know about that money, but I don't want to touch that yet," Solomon said. "I want to save it for my children and my mother." Mr. Carter went to his office and wrote out the check.

"Thank you very much. I appreciate your help," Solomon said, and he thanked Mr. Carter and went home.

Within a few months, Solomon had made enough money to pay off Mr. Carter. However, when he took the check to him, Mr. Carter refused to take it. Solomon looked at Mr. Carter and said, "But, sir, I borrowed this money from you, and I promised to pay it back in full. I am doing exactly as I promised. Please take your money; otherwise, I won't be satisfied."

"No, I can't take it. I want you to keep this money and use it for yourself. I gave it to you as a gift."

"Sir, when you gave me that money, I considered it a loan. I want to repay you."

"Every time I look at you, I see your father in you. He was a great man, and he did many good things for me. If it weren't for your father, I would have lost everything. I really want to help you, Solomon, but you have always refused my gifts, and so has your mother. Please don't try to repay me."

Solomon saw the tears in Mr. Carter's eyes and apologized profusely. Mr. Carter had always been there for his mother and him ever since his father had died. Solomon repeated, "I'm sorry, Solomon, but I can't take your money, and I will keep it that way. I don't care what you think or say. Take care of yourself."

With that Solomon went home.

A year into his job, after dropping off a customer one rainy afternoon, Solomon felt tired and was heading home to get some rest. He saw four gentlemen standing in the rain; one of them, whose name was Philippe, was flagging him down. He looked like a police officer. They were carrying a couple of black bags. His compassion got the better of him. He stopped, and three of them got in. Philippe was five feet nine with black hair, brown eyes, a bald head, and a fat build. He wore eyeglasses. He also was knock-kneed. He was a corrupt police officer who was also part of an armed gang. He took a good look at Solomon.

"Where are you guys headed?" he asked.

"Washington, DC," the guy in front answered.

"Oh, I'm sorry, I can't take you. I don't travel that far for fares."

"Please, we've been standing out here in the freezing rain for some time now. We'll pay you well. We'll even double your price if you take us. It's important that we get there soon; lots of people are waiting for us, and we are already running late," said the same gentlemen.

At that moment, the guy sitting at the far right behind Solomon was trying to pull out his gun, but the others quickly signaled him to put it back.

"If you take us, you won't regret it; today might even turn out to be one of your lucky days," the fellow with the gun said darkly as they made themselves comfortable.

Solomon quickly thought for a moment and replied, "You know what? I would like you guys to pay me up front before I take you all the way to DC."

"We'll use the meter to know how much to pay you, isn't that right?" the one in the front asked.

"Look, gentlemen, this is my cab. Don't preach law to me. Now I have a headache. I'm tired, and I just want to go home, but you told me you would pay me well, so I want to see if you guys are men of your word," Solomon said.

"All right, you got us. You can see how badly we want to get out of here," one of the men said. He took out a big bundle of cash and gave it to Solomon. "Now are you satisfied? Can you take us?" the same fellow asked.

"Sure." Without counting the money, Solomon quickly put it in his pocket. "It'd be my pleasure to drive you to your destination. What are your names?" Solomon asked. The man in the front seat said, "My name is Francis." Then he introduced his friends.

"The guy that flagged you down, his name is Philippe. He's a police officer, and we work together," Francis answered.

On the way to Washington, DC, Francis and his friends slept in silence. When they got to the address, Solomon woke them up. They thanked Solomon, but one of the men neglected to remove his bag from the cab. None of the other men noticed, nor did Solomon.

When Francis and his men got home, they celebrated—they had just robbed a bank successfully at the very spot where Solomon had picked them up. After the party they realized that one of the moneybags was missing. They quickly phoned Philippe and explained the situation, but they couldn't talk much because he was busy trying to cover the mess they had left behind.

After racking their brains, they concluded that they had left the moneybag in Solomon's taxi. They planned to find him and recover their money when the situation cooled down.

Meanwhile Solomon drove straight home that evening, parked his taxi, and took some Advil. He went straight to bed and woke up at 9:00 p.m.

Later he went out to his taxi to clean up the inside. In the trunk he found a strong, big, black holdall bag. Remembering the four men he'd driven to DC, he took out the bag and locked the trunk. He took the bag inside and tried to open it in order to determine the rightful owner. It was locked. Solomon tried several different codes in an attempt to open it but was unsuccessful. He sat down to think about what to do next. He decided to take the bag to the police department and let them deal with the situation. He took the bag to his taxi, and just as he started the car, a thought ran through his head: *Maybe this isn't a good idea.* He turned the car off and took the bag into the house. He then anxiously tried to open the bag to see what was inside it.

He grabbed a hammer to break the lock. After a few attempts, the lock yielded, and the bag cracked open. Inside was an array of various files. He removed the files, but what he saw underneath the files was shocking: bundles of cash tied in neat, thick stacks of one-hundred-dollar bills. He took out a bundle and smiled, breathing in the scent and savoring the delicate feel of the fresh money in his fingers.

Solomon quickly scanned through the three separate files. They contained personal information about the bank and all of its clients' personal banking information. After two hours of reading, he realized that the information was powerful, and the police would already be searching for the men who had stolen it.

Fear ran through Solomon's veins, and he decided to keep all the files and the money a secret—he would never give it to the authorities. He knew that if he returned them, he could be held as one of the robbers or an accomplice.

Only highly trusted officials of that banking institution would have been allowed access to the information he had, and if they were used improperly, it could destroy the entire bank and millions of its clients.

Suddenly Solomon found himself in a critical dilemma. He had to do something with the bag. He tried to think of someone he could trust to share the information with just in case he was harmed. Three people quickly came to his mind: his ex-wife, his mother, and Mr. Carter. After much thought he took his ex-wife out of the picture and concentrated on his mother and Mr. Carter.

Mr. Carter was his first choice, as Solomon had entrusted him with his money, and he hadn't touched it since. Then he thought about his mother; since she had given him life and stood by him all these years—during good times and bad times—she would sacrifice for him because of the love they shared. His decision was made. He decided to trust his mother rather than Mr. Carter. He didn't even think about counting the money; there was too much. He was also thinking about the quick money he could make from those documents.

Chapter 14

Solomon took out a few of the files and hid them under his bed. He rented a car and drove to Chicago. His mother, thrilled to see him, welcomed him with open arms. Solomon set his bags down on the floor. His mother hugged him tightly and kissed him; then she made him sit down while she rushed to get him something to drink.

"Are you hungry? I prepared some food earlier, and I still have some in the fridge," Clare said.

"Yes, please, Mom. I'm hungry."

Clare quickly set the dining table and brought the food out. Solomon ate and helped clean up the dishes before sitting with his mother in the living room.

"How is your taxi driving job going?"

"The job is great; I really like it. I look forward to it every day. It's a good job."

"I talked to your children just an hour ago, and they told me they miss you."

"Yeah, I miss them too. I've just been really busy with my job lately. I haven't had time to go visit them. I'll try to see them sometime this week. I did talk to them earlier today though."

"I don't care if you love your job or not, please stay close to your children. They are my grandchildren, and I love them just as I love you. I raised you by myself. I tried to be there for you every day. So if your children want to see you, don't turn your back on them. That's not the way I raised you. I also want to know my grandchildren better by spending more time with them."

"Why are you talking like that? I would never leave my children without a father." "I'm saying this because I know you're a lucky child. You've had many good things happen in your life, but you've destroyed them. There are people out there who are praying to be as lucky as you are. You should keep all the good things, stick with them, love them, and fight what is evil."

"Mom, I have a serious problem, and I need your help."

"Well, as your mother, I have been helping you since the day you were born until you grew up and became a man. I am grateful that you always trust me whenever you have a problem."

He paused and breathed deeply before continuing. "Mom, let me show you something very important."

Clare came over and Solomon opened the bag. When his mother saw what was inside, she fainted. Solomon tried to wake her, but she wasn't breathing. He thought that his mother had died. Frantic, he ran into her bedroom and hid the bag under her bed. He ran and called some of the neighbors for help. They came running to see what was going on.

When they entered the house, they saw Clare on the floor unconscious. One of the neighbors told Solomon to bring some ice-cold water. The jolting splash of cold water on her skin woke up Clare, to everyone's relief.

A neighbor brought Clare a glass of water. She took a sip and sat in her chair, glaring at Solomon. He came over to her and whispered, "Mom, it's all right; everything is going to be fine."

The neighbors stayed with her for an hour to make sure she was all right and comfortable. Some suggested that she see a doctor, but she told them she was fine. When all of her neighbors had left and Clare was sitting alone, she gave Solomon a terrible glare. Solomon got up and went to prepare a cup of tea for her. She took a sip then set it on the table and thanked him.

"What kind of document was in that bag you showed me earlier, and where did you get all that money?"

Solomon was surprised at his mother's questions.

"But, Mom, I thought when you saw the documents, you knew what they were, and that's why you fainted."

"Yes, I saw them and the money, but I can't remember the contents. That money is too much. I've never seen so much cash before."

Solomon went into his mother's bedroom to get the bag. He brought it out and set it in front of her. As soon he opened the bag, he changed his mind. He looked at his mother. "I don't want you to faint again." He retrieved a bucket of cold water from the kitchen and sat it down beside her.

"Don't be scared. I won't faint again. I don't know what happened, but trust me, it won't happen again."

Solomon carefully opened the bag while staring at his mother's face to make sure nothing went wrong. He took out one of the files and showed it to her. Clare opened it and quickly scanned through it. She then looked at the other files and asked, "Where did you get these documents and the money?"

Solomon explained. When Clare heard the story, she started to shake; fear trembled in her voice and flashed in her eyes.

"Solomon, I'm not with you on this. Have you lost your mind? Do you know what you're doing?"

"Yes, Mom. These documents contain top-secret information about our country's banking system. With this information you could destroy all of these people any time you want. I'm sure those four men had bad intentions for these documents and the money, so fate has allowed them to fall into my hands. But I have no intention of giving this information back to them or to the police."

"You must be joking. Are you trying to play with me?"

"No, Mom, I'm not. That's why I came all the way here to see you. I really do mean what I am saying. You are my mother, and I would never lie to you."

"Look, don't give me this crap! You have lied to me plenty of times. You never keep any of your promises, and don't make me start naming them. In fact, I don't even believe that somebody would just get into your taxi and leave such an important bag behind."

"Mom, you have to believe me. I wouldn't come all the way from New York just to make up stories to tell you."

"Listen, I am not saying that I don't believe you. All I am saying is that it's hard for me to understand how someone could just forget such an important bag in your taxi."

Solomon was silent for a moment, hesitant to pressure his mom.

Clare asked again, "Why won't you just take them to the police and tell them how you happened upon them? This information is too dangerous for me to have in my house. I don't want to get killed because of your stupidity."

"Nobody is going to die, and nobody is going to do anything to you," Solomon said.

Clare was just staring, wondering if she was still sane.

"Where are you planning to keep your trouble bag?"

"I brought the bag hoping that you would keep it for me, I want you to keep them, no matter what happens. If I die, then as long as they don't find this bag, I'll know that this money will make your life much easier. Look, Mom, this is a lot of money."

"Are you out of your mind? Do you know what you're saying? I'm not going to keep such a sensitive bag here." She started to shake with fear.

Solomon got up and went outside to stand on the porch. He watched the streets, hoping that his mother would calm down and understand him. Cars passed slowly, and a cold wind blew as Clare wondered how life had taken such an unexpected turn.

Chapter 15

He returned five minutes later and knelt down in front of her. "Mom, I love you, and the last thing I would ever do is put your safety at risk. You are my mother, and I will do everything in my power to protect you. But please don't let me down; I have nobody else to go to."

Clare stared at Solomon and paused for a moment before speaking. "The files and money belong to the city bank, and I know that it has taken those gentlemen many years of planning in a high-risk environment to get them. I think they'll do whatever it takes to get them back. I love you very much, and I don't want to lose you. Suppose the police come here looking for these documents?"

"Mom, there are hundreds of homes in this neighborhood. Do you really believe they would think of coming to this house to look for the things that went missing from New York? There's a good chance that those fellows don't remember what I look like. It was raining very hard that day, and they slept for most of the drive to Washington, DC. All they were thinking about was getting to their appointment. I just want you to trust me, that's all."

"Sorry, dear, I think these documents and the money are very important to the bank, and they deserve to get them back."

Solomon was desperate. "Even if I turn these documents over to the police, you never know what they might do with them. It's hard to trust anyone, even the police—one of the men didn't get into the car, and I found out during the drive that he was a police officer. Besides, only trusted officials in the bank would have access to this information. If they realize that we have seen these files, we will be in serious trouble, and who knows what might happen next. That's why we need to think of a strong solution."

Clare was touched by the look in her son's eyes. She didn't want to disappoint him.

"So what do you want me to do with them? Where do you expect me to keep them?"

"Let me think."

Solomon paced back and forth with his finger on his lips.

A few minutes later, Clare said, "Take that bucket of water out of my living room and put it back where you got it. While you're there, grab me some more tea…" She paused before continuing. "I will help you in any way that I can. I promise."

Solomon believed his mother, and he was relieved. "I knew you were the greatest mother on the planet." He gave her a big kiss.

"What do you really want to do with your life?"

"I want to be a rich man with morals and principles. I hate other people being treated with injustice. Perhaps God put this bag into my hands in order to help protect innocent people from who knows what. You just have to help me and leave the rest in God's hands. I'm happy to have a woman like you as a mother, and I mean it sincerely. I know I have lied to you and let you down many times, but I promise you that I will keep praying to God so that he will keep smiling down on you."

"Have you come to any conclusion about where you're going to keep this bag of money?" Clare asked.

"I was thinking of keeping it in your bedroom."

"Do you want to keep it in the wall safe or under the bed?"

"I have an idea. I'll be right back." Solomon went to his mother's back yard to check it out. He came up with a bright idea of digging a hole among his mother flower garden, stashing the bag in it, then covering it. That way nobody would get suspicious about anything.

"Mom, I have an idea. I'll make a hole among your flower and then we will put the bag in the hole and plaster it with cement. Then we can both forget about it forever."

"I think that might be a good idea," Clare agreed.

That night he bought some cement and digging equipment from a hardware store. He dug a hole in the middle of the garden, Plaster inside with cement, waited until it dried. Solomon wrap two black garbage bags around the moneybag and place it inside. He covered the bag with some of the dirt he had dug earlier before plastering it with cement. He then carefully put the top soil on top the cement and planted the flowers back.

"I think all your thoughts and conversations are based on money," Clare said. "You love money more then you love yourself. I know you'll do anything for money. Everybody loves money, but most people think about getting their money in a responsible manner, rather than going around trying to hurt other people for their money. You misused the power that came with all the money you've made in the past, and it has brought you back to zero. I think money doesn't like you."

"You're right, Mom; I love money very much. Nothing is going to change my thoughts about money. I'm sure that money loves me too, and I will get money again. I understand where you're coming from, and I will take your advice seriously. At least I'm lucky to still have you around as my best friend and my mother. I pray that you live long, so you can witness how great I will become."

That was their last night together. The next day she drove him to the airport. The following day Solomon took the remaining documents to Velma Quilmes's house; she was a well-respected money launderer and business associate of Solomon's. After a few questions, Velma put her boys to work, and they quickly prepared fake credit cards and debit cards with the documents' information. They were able to withdraw close to six million dollars before the bank noticed anything.

Solomon told Velma to keep his share of the money When the time was right, he would come back for it. Velma was trustworthy, and he knew it. He left the documents with Velma, but after she and her men noticed the police closing in on them, she destroyed all the evidence.

For Solomon, everything was back to normal.

***

Sgt. Sten Williamson, assistant director of the New York Special Organized Crime Unit for the FBI met with his staff to go over the details of the robbery that evening. His two sons had been killed during the heist. One had been a New York police officer on duty and the other a teller at the bank where some sensitive documents and a large amount of money had been stolen. Sten was six feet tall, bald, and clean-shaven with a mustache and a white complexion.

Sten son Justin happened to be the partner of Philippe Venier, who Sten arrested base on reliable information received from tipsters. But Philippe was cooperating and he was sharing information with the FBI.

Philippe had actually killed Justin while helping the robber to escape. He shot two others who he believed saw what had happened.

Everyone had sprung into action to retrieve the missing information and money.

Sten called a quick meeting, and the room was full. He told them to go back to Philippe's house to try to find out who his friends were and where his cell phone was. With it they could find out whom he had talked to that week. Then Sten ordered that they seize any computerized information they found. That way they could contact his friends and relatives to have them brought in for questioning. When the meeting was over, he sent them on their way to do what they had been told.

Philippe's family and friends were all taken in for questioning. Anyone who had been working that day was also questioned. Even the employees at the restaurant he had called to order a pizza were questioned.

The FBI was taking no chances, and the bureau did everything it could to locate the documents. Everyone was prepared for the worst. The interrogation rooms were filled to capacity as the officers strained to squeeze out information.

They didn't have any luck with the sketch that had been drawn using the information Philippe had given them. It was suggested that a copy of the sketch be sent to various locations around the state. The individual agencies also took copies to all of the police stations in their jurisdictions. It was costing them a lot of money, but that didn't matter; it was too important to find those robbers. Sten would not rest until they were found.

When the sketch gave no leads, they decided to try all the prisons around the country, but this still gave them nothing. Nobody on the streets was of any help, and they had no success with their own database. They went back to see Philippe, but that didn't help either. Sten decided to bring in his best detective. His name was Aaron Skokie. He was a New York native with a mean frown that always made him look serious. He had great respect within his department and had solved lots of difficult cases.

Chapter 16

When Aaron arrived he was briefed on everything that had been done; afterward he decided to speak with Philippe himself. He asked Philippe to take his time and tell him everything that had happened. As Philippe went over his story, he listened closely. When Philippe finished, the detective asked him to close his eyes and picture the cab driver. Philippe did this, and then Aaron asked him to look at the sketch and try to refine it. With that new information, they sent out an updated sketch. Philippe felt it looked more like Solomon, the taxi driver. There was hope that they might be more successful this time.

Philippe had many friends who all had extended families, and the FBI was not taking any chances on letting any of them leave without questioning them first. The problem was that the officers were severely demoralized after the death of Sten's two sons and the innocent victims who were murdered. Only Philippe knew the truth.

Eventually there was some good news. They had found a match. When Sten received a copy of the photograph, they took it directly to Philippe. When he saw the photo, he confirmed Solomon as the individual who had been driving the taxi with the three robbers.

"Are you sure? Look at it again," Sten ordered anxiously.

Philippe looked at it again and said, "Yes, that's him. He has the documents and the money. Find him."

Sten asked that more officers to be assigned to monitor Philippe. He wasn't to be trusted.

Everyone scrambled to get as much information as possible. It was a difficult task, but every officer wanted to prove to the chief that they were ready for promotion.

A couple of hours later, the information Sten wanted was on his desk. He went over it, and another meeting was called. The officers were asked for any ideas, and Aaron suggested, "The only thing we can do is put his picture on television so that the American public can help find him. That would probably be the fastest way to find him."

Sten didn't really buy that idea.

"If we put his picture on television, and he finds out about it, he could hide, destroy the evidence, or even escape the country. We're also not really sure if he's the person we're searching for, and he could just be an innocent taxi driver."

There was a reward posted for Solomon's capture, and the law enforcement officers wanted in on it. They put in more hours on the job to try to find him, but they were warned that he was wanted alive, not dead. They spent a lot of time on the streets, at the shopping malls, and in nightclubs showing his picture to everyone. They worked closely with police offices in Washington, DC.

Suspecting the police were probably looking for him, Solomon decided not to drive his cab. Instead he got one of his friends to drive the taxi for him while he stayed at home enjoying himself, eating, drinking, and being merry. He also attempted to change all his personal information, starting with the bank and phone company, and also warned his driver never to say anything to anybody about him, whether they knew him or not. He had total trust in his driver, so he didn't worry about him at all.

Thinking it prudent to change his address as well, one afternoon Solomon found a nice building in a secluded location and rented a two-bedroom apartment in it. He didn't tell his ex-wife anything anymore. He didn't have a phone. Instead he just used the public phone on the street. He felt quite safe and assured that no one could find him.

However, the authorities were hunting for him like a hungry lion on the prowl. They were checking any information that would lead to Solomon's capture, and they even went to various financial agencies to see if that would get them any information on him. They checked the telephone companies but had no success. They were getting frustrated.

But Solomon made one fatal mistake.

Nobody was getting anywhere in locating Solomon, until they contacted the taxi companies. Solomon had forgotten to change the information on his driver's license, so they were able to get his license plate number, address, and phone number.

With this new information, Sten put together a SWAT team. Soon they were dispatched to the address on his driver's license. They surrounded it and sealed off all possible escape routes. They broke down the door and entered, but the house was empty. It was obvious that nobody lived there anymore. They found the owner of the building and showed him the picture of Solomon, asking if he knew him or his whereabouts.

"Oh yes, I know Solomon. He's a nice man. He's very friendly. My wife and grandchildren love him very much. He left about two months ago. We weren't happy about his leaving because we knew we would miss him. That's why we've never rented it out to anybody else. We're looking for a nice person just like him. He never told us where he was moving to or his phone number. Why are you searching for him? What did he do?" the old man asked.

Frustrated, they decided to find the taxi. New York was full of officers in the street searching for him. They inspected every taxi they laid eyes on and went to every taxi stand in the city. They questioned every driver and showed them the photo of Solomon; but he was not very popular, and most of the drivers never really knew him. But the officers didn't give up.

Meanwhile Solomon was keeping a low profile. He kept in constant contact with his mother and Mr. Carter by using public pay phones.

One day the police found his ex-wife based on a tip. They asked for her cooperation. She agreed and answered their questions as best she could, but the one thing they couldn't get from her was Solomon's whereabouts. She did tell them that he called all the time to talk to his children, and she was able to give them his mother's information.

Sten was very pleased with the information. When they returned to their offices, they arranged to have a wiretap put on Mary's line. Two FBI agents, Dan Johnson and Wilcox smithy, quickly flew to Chicago and went to the address given for Solomon's mother. When they knocked on the door, she wasn't home, so they waited in their car across the street.

***

Clare had spent the day with her family. She was so tired that evening when she returned home that she drove past her house. In doing so she noticed a car parked across the street but didn't make anything of it. However, the officers didn't see her—they had fallen asleep. She parked her car in the garage and entered the house. As she was tired, Clare didn't turn on any lights and went straight to bed. By the time the officers woke up, there were still no signs of life.

Den suggested, "Let's go check the house again. Maybe somebody is inside, and they didn't hear us knocking on the door."

Wilcox agreed. They got out of the car and crossed the street. They knocked very hard on the door, but Clare was fast asleep and didn't hear them. They kept knocking and calling out, "Is anybody home?" Finally she woke up. Clare mused, *Who would be knocking at my door at this time of the night?* She looked at her watch and saw that it was early yet. She got up, washed her face, and put on some clothes. She then turned on the light and looked out; she saw two well-dressed men and opened the door.

"What do you want?"

"We're sorry to disturb you." The officers took out their ID badges and showed them to her.

"We're FBI agents from New York, and we want to talk to you," Wilcox said. "May we come inside?"

"Well, gentleman, I would like to call our community leader so he can be here to listen to whatever you want to talk about. I won't talk to you people without seeing him, and I will not invite you into my home because I don't know who you are. You have guns, right?" she asked.

Wilcox and Den stared at each other and smiled. "Yes we do. We have to carry one everywhere we go because we are FBI agents. Look, we aren't here to hurt you. We only want to talk to you and ask you a few questions. We don't want to involve any others in this."

She stared at Wilcox and then stared at Den and said, "OK, I will let you in but just for a few minutes."

They took out a tape recorder and set out their notebooks and pens. Wilcox took out Solomon's photo and showed it to her. "Do you know the man in this photo?"

She grabbed the photograph and looked at it, telling them, "He is my son, Solomon. What happened? What did he do?"

"Did he ever tell you anything with regard to some documents or money, or did he say anything that sounded strange to you?"

"Oh yes, he is my son, and we talk about everything. He tells me things, but don't expect me to tell you anything we talked about!" she replied.

"When was the last time you talked to him?" Den asked.

"About two weeks ago," she answered.

"Where did he call you from?"

"From New York."

"Do you know where he lives now?" Wilcox asked.

"Yes, of course, he is my son. How can I not know where he lives?"

"Can you give us his address?" Den asked.

"Why? So you can go and arrest him?" she asked.

"Yes, because he's wanted by the FBI for questioning. If he tells us what we need to know, then we will let him go," Wilcox told her.

With that she gave the agents Solomon's address. Wilcox compared the address they had with the one she had given them, and it was the same.

"Sorry, but this is the address we already checked, and nobody lives there anymore," Wilcox said.

"Well, that is the only address I have for him, and that is the number I call him at."

When the officers heard this, one of them took out his cell phone and called Sten. They gave the phone number to their boss to check out.

"During your last conversation, did he tell you he was planning on moving or staying at a hotel? Was he planning to move to another state?" Den asked.

"Well, he didn't say anything to me about any of those things. He told me that he loved New York and was doing well with his business. I moved here from New York couple of years ago, and I have only visited the city twice since then. The last time was when he invited me to see his new house. Since then we've only talked on the phone," she told them.

"Did he come here to see you in the last few days?" Den asked.

"No," she answered.

"Do you know the names of any of his close friends who might know his whereabouts?" Wilcox asked.

"None that I know of."

"How would you describe your son? He has a criminal record."

"I would tell anyone who asked me that he is a very fine young man. Even though he has made mistakes in the past, he has been keeping to himself, driving his taxi, and staying away from old friends because he is a weak-minded person. He will do anything to help his friends, and that is what leads him into trouble. I love him dearly, and I believe he is a great human being. I am grateful to God for having such a son," she declared proudly.

Chapter 17

Den and Wilcox kept prodding her for information. "If your son had any problems, or if he had something important on his mind and wanted to discuss it with someone, who do you think he would go talk to first? Who do you think he would trust above anyone?"

"No doubt it's me. As his mother I know he trusts me more than anyone, and I have never disappointed him as I only want to see good things happen to him."

They thanked her and left. Den and Wilcox flew back to New York and reported on what they had found to their Sten. They asked if any more information had been discovered from the telephone number that Solomon's mother had given them.

"We called the phone company to get additional information, but again it is the same information we already have, so it didn't make any difference. Give me a few minutes, and I'll examine your notes and tape and get back to you."

Sten went back to his office and listened to the taped interview with Solomon's mother. He made some notes and then came out to Den and Wilcox.

"I want you guys to tape any phone calls and listen to her conversations. I also want you to keep close watch on her house and pay close attention to the people who go in and out. Install cameras all around the house, and keep in close contact with me every hour," Sten ordered.

Den and Wilcox drove back to Chicago in a water truck stocked with computers, monitors, and all the equipment they might need to obtain as much information as they possibly could. They parked as close as they could to Clare's house and pretended to be city workers repairing water pipes under the street. They were now working closely with the Chicago police department. Den and Wilcox stayed in the truck and sent a couple of other officers out to act as the workers. They informed the neighbors that they would be working on damaged water pipes. They also told them that they didn't know how long it would take to complete the repairs.

Meanwhile the hunt for Solomon was escalating. More police officers worked the streets in an all-out effort to locate him and get the reward money. One day two undercover detectives turned onto Queens Boulevard in Queens and happened to see a taxi parked outside an apartment building. They decided to check out the license plate and were surprised and delighted to find the taxi they had all been searching for. They quickly stopped the car and approached the taxi with their guns in hand.

As they neared the taxi, they saw a longhaired man sitting in the driver's seat. "Who is driving this taxi?" they demanded.

"I am," the man replied.

"Who is the owner of the taxi?" they asked again.

"It's my taxi," he replied.

"What is your name, sir?" they asked.

"Gerald Morris Peterson," he answered. But at this he got angry and asked, "Who do you think you people are—asking me all kinds of stupid questions. What's going on?"

One of the officers told him to shut up and get out of the car. They stood with their guns pointed at Peterson and warned him to cooperate. They told him that if he tried to run, they would not hesitate to shoot him.

When Peterson saw the look on their faces, he could see that they meant business, so he slowly got out of the car. They handcuffed him and put him in the back of their car. The officers called a tow truck and arranged for the taxi to be towed back to Sten's office. On the ride back, they asked him, "What were you doing sitting in front of that building?"

"I was waiting for a customer," Peterson replied.

***

Back at the office, they took the driver directly to Philippe's cell and asked him to identify the man.

Philippe looked at Peterson carefully and told them that he wasn't the person they were searching for. They escorted Philippe to where the towed taxi sat and asked, "Does this taxi look familiar to you? Is it like the one that the robbers took that day?"

Philippe had handcuffs on both his wrists and ankles, but he walked around the taxi slowly. He looked through the open door and checked the backseat before he announced,

"This is the right taxi!"

"Are you sure this is the taxi that was used that day?" Sten asked.

"Yes, I'm sure," replied Philippe.

"What makes you so sure? You told us you were very busy that day and were not paying attention," Sten said, starring directly into his eyes.

"I know it because of the little blue spot on the left corner of the plate," he told them.

Sten was exhilarated at the prospect of closing in on his suspect. He ordered Philippe to be taken back to his cell, and they went back to interview Peterson.

After interrogating him about his personal details, Sten sat down, looked at Peterson, and paused for a moment before saying, "The information you're providing us with had better be 100 percent truth, or you could go to jail for a long time. Your children will grow up without their father, and your wife won't see you for a long time—your life will be ruined. Now who is the owner of the taxi you're driving? I know that it's not yours."

While Sten said this, one of his men entered and handed him a file. Sten quickly went through the information. Solomon had transferred ownership to Gerald Morris Peterson, and he was indeed the rightful owner of the taxi.

Even though Peterson was telling the truth, Sten was still not convinced that Peterson was telling him the whole truth.

"Look, I think you know Solomon and that you work for him, and I think he changed all the documents in order to stay hidden. Why would you protect him and let yourself suffer the heat if you have a beautiful wife and children waiting at home for you? You had better take some time and think things over."

Sten walked out, closed the door behind him, and asked one of his men what information they had on Peterson.

"We have his driver's license, his social security, and all the information from his wallet."

Sten returned to the room and closed the door. He sat down and looked at Peterson.

"Well, tell me everything you know, and I promise that you will have complete immunity from anything that might happen afterward. I will also make sure that your family is protected, but only if you're telling me the truth," he said.

Peterson thought for a minute and then made up his mind to rat out Solomon for personal reasons. He couldn't really afford to lose everything that he had just to cover up for the man he worked for. So he poured out everything he knew about Solomon. Sten listened carefully and took notes.

"Do you take all the money you make for a day to his home, or do you meet at a specified location?" he asked.

"I don't know where he lives or his phone number. As I told you earlier, we meet at a specified location every night at midnight so I can give him his money. That's the only time I see him," Peterson stated.

"Does that mean he's supposed to meet you there tonight?" Sten asked. He was closing in. His moment of triumph was coming.

"I'm pretty sure he will be waiting for his money at midnight because he has never missed a night," Peterson replied.

"OK, this is what I want you to do for us: we will follow you to your usual meeting place, and once we capture him, you'll be a free man but only if we have your full cooperation and you do what we tell you to do," Sten told him.

"But, sir, before I help you, I want you to tell me why you're looking for him," he said.

"We have some important questions we need to ask him. He might not be the person we are looking for, but we won't know until we have an opportunity to speak to him. Once we've done that, he may even be able to leave as a free man. It's very important to us and our government that we find this man, and you can be a great help to us in this task," Sten said.

Chapter 18

Sten quickly put together the necessary team and wired Peterson up. His team was dressed and armed to the teeth.

"We'll take you back to where the detectives took you from in your own taxi, but one of my men will be driving. Once we reach the location, we will seal the surrounding area completely, and when he arrives we will close in on him."

Sten then said, "Are you ready to help me get this man or what?"

It was a dark, starless night. As midnight arrived the officers quickly scattered around and took cover. Peterson stood to the side of the taxi with his hands on top of the roof waiting for Solomon.

Solomon wasn't feeling comfortable. He felt that something wasn't right. He knew something bad was going to happen if he met Peterson at their usual spot. As he got closer, he noticed strangers walking around in the area and decided he would forget about meeting with Peterson to get his money.

He went home and called his mother from a pay phone a short distance from his house.

"How are you coming along with everything?" he asked his mother.

"Things are not too good here. A few days ago, two men from the FBI came here and asked me questions about you. They couldn't really tell me why they were looking for you, but they said you were of interest to the government and that you were wanted for questioning. They even asked me if you had come to see me at all. I told them that you hadn't and that I didn't know where you lived, but they pressured me and I gave them your address."

Solomon inhaled sharply and exhaled slowly. He could handle this. "Mom, have you noticed anything strange happening in your neighborhood lately?" he asked.

"The only thing strange around here is that our sewer system was damaged, and they have a big van parked on the other side of the street opposite my house. They have been here for quite a while now, and the pipes are still not repaired. Everything else is the same."

"Thanks, Mom. I'll talk to you soon." Solomon hung up the phone.

While their conversation was being taped, Wilcox and Den in the van outside of Clare's house traced the location of the phone. Den passed this information along to Sten in New York, who knew that Solomon would not be showing up where they were waiting. He called the number that Solomon had called from, but there was no answer. He decided to leave some of his men at their present location and took another team to the location of the pay phone that they had traced. The handset and door were dusted for fingerprints. They looked around to make sure there were no other clues lying around, but Solomon was long gone.

Peterson was returned to his jail cell with the threat that he would be staying there until the case was solved, unless he had some other information that might help them in their efforts. Sten arranged for some of his men to keep an eye on the pay phone in case Solomon used it again; he sent the rest back to check out whose fingerprints they had collected from the phone booth. Sure enough, when the results of the fingerprint testing came back, Solomon's were among them, so they had confirmation that he had used that pay phone. They maintained surveillance on that location. Sten wanted Solomon so badly he could taste it, especially when he thought about the death of his boys. They couldn't afford to miss any clues.

Solomon was worried. He knew the police were hungrily searching for him. He started smoking cigarettes and drinking to lessen his stress; meanwhile, the stress was keeping him up at night, and the lack of rest was fraying his nerves. He had to keep thinking about every move he made, and each time he left his house, he was afraid the police would find him.

Solomon called Mr. Carter to wish him a happy birthday, but he was told to hang up and not to call him again. Solomon asked, "What happened? Why are you talking like this?"

"The FBI came to see me. They threatened my family and me. They think I know where you are, and they told me that I should turn you in; otherwise, they will put my family and me in jail until I tell them your whereabouts. I believe they are monitoring my phone calls. That's why I don't want to talk too much. If you want, I can meet you at our old spot at our usual time so we can talk."

Solomon agreed to meet with him, relieved that in a world of sharks, he could trust Mr. Carter.

Mr. Carter's phone was being monitored, but he had already left to meet Solomon before the FBI could get to his house to follow him. They waited outside his house for him to return.

When Mr. Carter arrived, Solomon was already there and looking around carefully to make sure nobody had followed him. Mr. Carter parked his car a little distance away. When they met, they shook hands, hugged each other, and went to sit down on one of the benches.

"So tell me why the police are looking for you. I want you to tell me everything so we can find a way to help you out," Mr. Carter told him.

Solomon saw his concern, so he decided to tell him everything except where he had hidden the bag, but Mr. Carter was not interested in hearing that. He listened quietly to Solomon's story and told him to keep his courage if he felt that the documents and the money meant that much to him. "However," Mr. Carter said, "they are only papers, and it might be better for you to return the documents so the FBI will leave you alone."

"But, sir, if I give them back what they want, they won't let me go. Instead they'll probably kill me because the documents are too important for ordinary people to see. My choice is to keep the documents and the money so that millions of other people will be free of threat from a hostile criminal," he told Mr. Carter.

"Well, son, whatever you choose to do, I'll support you. As I told you earlier, I would like you to try very hard to keep my family and me out of this. My family and I have a lot to care for, and we have worked very hard to bring things to the state they are in now. We can't afford to lose our business over something like this. Now if you'll please excuse me." He walked back to his car and drove away.

Solomon took out a cigarette and thought about his situation. He knew he was in deep trouble, and whether he turned the money and the documents in or not, he would still have to face the consequences. He finished his cigarette and started his walk home. He was scared to think what would happen to him when he was caught. Suddenly an idea came to mind: he would leave the country and go to Stockholm. There he wouldn't have to worry about the FBI. He thought about all of his old connections and which of his friends would be able to help him get a passport.

He decided to go and see his old friend Jack. He managed to connect with his former best friend and tell him what he needed. Jack who was still living the fast life knew the business and the right people to approach in order to get Solomon what he wanted.

The wheels were in motion. Jack took him to a forger he knew. This man quickly prepared him a fake passport. He gave Solomon his personal guarantee that he would be able to travel out of the country without any problems. Solomon returned home and packed his suitcases. He sent Jack to buy him an airline ticket for a flight scheduled to leave that same night. Solomon was ecstatic; he hugged his friend and thanked him profusely.

They both got into a taxi and rode to the airport. Once there Solomon ran to join the queue that was waiting. When he presented his ticket and passport, the attendant looked at them and gave them back. He successfully boarded the plane that would take him to Frankfurt, Germany. His plan was to purchase a train ticket in Germany and continue his trip to Sweden.

***

Six months passed. Solomon's mother had been spending the day with her extended family. While she was gone, Den and Wilcox broke into her house to install a hidden camera and microphone. Now they could hear and see everything that went on and felt they wouldn't miss any important information that might be discussed. They knew she was the one Solomon trusted the most, and through her they believed they would eventually find him.

Meanwhile Solomon had settled in Stockholm. He had found himself a job rather quickly. He called Jack and told him all the good things about Europe: the people, the food, and everything else he enjoyed. Solomon wrote a postcard to Mr. Carter on which he wrote his new cell phone number.

Chapter 19

When Solomon first arrived in Stockholm, he called his mother, and they had a short conversation. He didn't call her again because he wanted to keep his location secret so he could stay safe and move on with his life.

Back home the FBI was getting increasingly desperate to find him. When they learned that Mr. Carter had been in contact with Solomon, they arrested him in front of his wife and children and took him to jail. They questioned him extensively about Solomon's whereabouts, but Mr. Carter refused to tell them. They applied for a search warrant from a judge and thoroughly searched his house, turning it upside down like rabid animals until they found the postcard from Solomon.

Now that they knew he was in Europe and had his cell phone number, they came down hard on Mr. Carter. Sten got angry and started physically abusing Mr. Carter; they showed him what they had found in his house. Mr. Carter finally broke down and told them about Solomon.

He also told them about his friend Jack. He was the only person who knew Solomon's new address. It was reasoned that they could probably find Solomon through him.

They kept Mr. Carter in his cell, and with the information he had given them, they went to arrest Jack. They weren't going to give Mr. Carter any more chances to lie to them.

Jack's apartment was searched inside and out, but Jack was smart—he didn't keep anything he had received from Solomon. They questioned Jack; they even tortured him in their attempt to wear him down. They left him in a cell, naked, with no sheets.

They attempted to trace the telephone number they had found on the postcard from Solomon. They had sent it to one of their departments to find out the name and address of the owner of the phone. They continued their interrogation of Jack, who clenched his teeth and endured the misery. He had loved Solomon since their childhood days back in Chicago, and he had always been a trustworthy friend.

Mr. Carter's family didn't even know where he was. They tried calling the NYPD office, but no one would give them any information. Mrs. Carter was confused and upset, growing more desperate by the day. Frantic, she called her lawyer, Collins Needier, and told him everything that had been happening. Mr. Collins took over the case and was able to locate where Mr. Carter had been taken. He demanded that his client be released at once, but he was told that it wasn't possible. Mr. Collins got angry and threatened that he was prepared to take the case to court, but they were not intimidated. They told him to take the case to any level he wanted, but Mr. Carter had lied to the FBI before, and they were not prepared to allow him to take their office for granted. They were investigating a serious crime, and he would be freed when they felt it was safe to do so. Mr. Collins said he would see them in court because they had no right to keep his client imprisoned and from seeing his family.

Sten finally had a name and address for the phone number they found on the postcard. It was for a man named James Horace who lived in Stockholm. Sten flew to Stockholm with some of his men; with the help of the Swedish special police force, he went directly to the address, but the apartment was empty.

Sten decided they should get more information on this James Horace. With the help of the Swedish authorities, they tried to obtain information from the phone company and various credit card companies, but they couldn't find a match.

When Solomon first arrived in Frankfurt, Germany, he had arranged to obtain another false document, which he used to enter Sweden. As soon as he had used the information on this document to get his apartment and phone, he knew that it would be easy for anyone to find him. So he tore the document up and moved to a better apartment, using the information that was contained in his fake American passport. He hadn't registered with the Swedish government, because when he had spoken to his mother, she said the best way to apply for Swedish citizenship was to link himself to his great-grandparents.

Sten gave all of the information, including photographs, to the Swedish authorities. He also left some of his men behind to continue the search for Solomon while he flew back to the United States. He was even angrier now than he had been before. He was a man on fire, desperate to solve the case. Furious, he went straight to Philippe's cell. He beat him and screamed that now was the time for him to tell the truth; otherwise, he would kill Philippe himself.

Philippe was scared and didn't know what to do. He had never seen Sten so out of control. Even his men were scared of what he might do. Unfortunately Philippe couldn't tell him anything more about what had happened that day because he had already told him the truth. Sten didn't care. Philippe's mistake had created all of the problems and laid them directly at his door, and he was the one who had the other government officials on his back on a daily basis.

***

Clare carried on with her life with no fear of anything at all. She was doing exactly as her son had told her to do. They still had Jack and

Mr. Carter in a cell, as well as Philippe, and they were prepared to arrest anyone who got in the way of their investigation.

Mr. Carter's lawyer had gone to court in an attempt to have his client released, but the FBI presented convincing evidence to the judge along with reasons why they felt Mr. Carter should remain in their custody. Nonetheless the judge ordered for Mr. Carter's release unless they could prove he was the kind of man they said he was.

Mr. Carter was released, but Sten warned him that they would continue to watch every move he made, and the smallest mistake would be one he would regret. Without saying anything, Mr. Carter turned and walked out of the courtroom with his lawyer.

***

With the information he received from his mother about relatives who lived in Sweden, Solomon was able to process his documents and was granted Swedish citizenship. He was now legally in Sweden. He found himself a job with a cleaning company that catered to offices, churches, and individual residences. He learned more and more about the city. One day he decided to return to driving a taxi. He had learned the language, and he knew his way around. He was enjoying every day and believed that the Swedish authorities would protect him, should the American authorities ever find him.

A few months later, when Solomon hadn't heard from his friend Jack, who he had been planning to invite to come live with him in Sweden, he tried calling his house from a public telephone, but there was no answer. Solomon decided to send him a letter. In it he included his address and phone number as well as a photo of himself. He told his friend to write him back or call him as soon as he received the letter. Solomon used his friend Damson's address and phone number as though it was his.

The FBI officer in charge of checking Jack's mail wasted no time when it arrived. He contacted Sten and gave him the information in the letter. Sten asked him to bring it to the office right away and sent a helicopter to pick him up. Sten and his men took a flight to Sweden the same night. They went at once to the address while the Swedish police obtained more information on Solomon.

Chapter 20

When they arrived with a SWAT team, they surrounded the building and closed off all possible escape routes. Sten used a microphone to plead with the people in the house to come out at once; otherwise, they would be forced to break in. As soon as Solomon's friend Damson heard the commotion outside and the sound of the helicopter flying overhead, he quickly opened the window to see what was going on. Damson could see the police pointing guns toward his house.

When the police saw him opening the window, they called out in Swedish, warning him to come out at once with his hands on top of his head. Damson complied and came out of the house scared, shaking, and wondering why they wanted to arrest him. The police quickly ran over to him and handcuffed him. When Sten came to see him, he was stunned to see that they had the wrong man. They asked for his name, and it wasn't Solomon. They piled into the house to search, but the only thing they found was the strong smell of marijuana. They brought him back inside his house and removed the handcuffs. They fetched him a glass of water to drink. He sat down in his chair breathing heavily.

"We're sorry. It was a mistake, but we need your cooperation. If you tell us the truth, we will let you go free; but if you lie to us, we will arrest you for smoking and possession of marijuana, and you will go to jail."

They quickly wrote down his name, date of birth, and all of his other personal information. While the police were checking his identity, Sten took out Solomon's photo and showed it to him. The man's eyes went wide in surprise.

"Do you know this individual?"

"Yes, I know him. He is my friend. What did he do?"

"He wrote to one of his friends in the United States and gave your address and phone number. He sent this photo. That's why we came to your house."

When Damson heard this, he agreed to cooperate. He gave Solomon's address and phone number to Sten and freely told him everything he knew about Solomon. Sten was so pleased he almost hugged Damson, but instead handed him one of his business cards and told him to give him a call as soon as he heard from Solomon.

Early the next morning, they surrounded the building where they believed they'd find Solomon. Sten warned the men not to hurt him because he was more important to them alive. While Solomon was fast asleep, heavily armed officers broke down his door and charged into the apartment. When he heard the noise, he tried to jump out the window, but it was too late; the police were already on him.

They threw him to the ground in his shorts and T-shirt and handcuffed him. They threw a blanket around him and escorted him downstairs to a waiting car. Sten was ecstatic; Solomon was finally in their possession after they had spent so much time and money trying to locate him.

When they returned to the offices of the Swedish authorities, Sten told them they would be extraditing Solomon to the United States.

However, when they checked Solomon's identification, they found that he was now a Swedish citizen. He was placed in protective custody with the Swedish authorities and told that his trial would be carried out under Swedish law. He would not be returning to the States to stand trial.

Things were getting very complicated for Sten. The Swedish government wanted copies of the evidence and all of the written information that had been gathered regarding Solomon's crime. Sten was confident, because as far as he was concerned, Solomon had been born in the United States and should be tried under American law. He quickly met with the Swedish chief of security and tried to convince him to take Solomon back to the United States because he was born there to American parents. After much consideration the chief of security agreed; he told Sten they had a deal. They released Solomon to Sten and apologized for the misunderstanding. Once Sten had Solomon back in his possession, he didn't want to waste any time in getting Solomon back to New York.

On the plane back to the New York, Sten allowed Solomon to have enough rest. "Hi, Solomon. My name is Sten, and it has been a great nightmare knowing about you. I took over this case because it is very personal to me, and you will know why later. We will have a serious conversation once we arrive at my office, and during that time I will require your full cooperation. But now I want you to rest enough because it will be a long conversation."

Solomon just stared at Sten as he made himself comfortable and ready to sleep.

***

Back at the office in New York, Sten savored the moment he had been waiting for so long. He brought both Solomon and Philippe into the interrogation room—no one else.

Sten turned to Philippe and said, "Look at this man. Is he the person you told us about?"

Immediately Philippe answered, "Yes, this is the man."

Then Sten turned to Solomon and asked, "Do you know this fellow?"

"Not at all," Solomon answered.

When he heard this, Philippe angrily said, "Don't lie here. Do you have any idea what you have put my family and me through? You and your friends killed those people in the bank—I saw you guys. Just tell them the truth, so we can all be free and go back to our normal lives."

"I don't know what you're talking about. I don't know you. I've never seen you before. I certainly would remember if I did," Solomon told him.

"So are you saying that you've never driven a taxi before?" Sten asked calmly.

"Oh yes, I owned a taxi. That was my job," Solomon replied as he took out a cigarette and lit it.

"Thank you for your cooperation, Philippe. You may go now," Sten told him.

Philippe stood up and asked, "Does this mean I can go home to my family now since you have this man?"

Sten turned and angrily asked, "Do you think I'm joking here? Don't you know my children were killed because of this psycho here? Take this stupid fool back to his jail cell!" he ordered.

Sten then asked Peterson to be brought to him. He had to get dressed before they brought him. When he came into the interrogation room, Sten asked Solomon, "Do you know this man?"

"Yes, he's my driver," Solomon replied.

"Is this true?" he asked Peterson.

"Yes, he's my boss. He is one of the kindest and sweetest people I've ever met," Peterson replied.

Sten then told his aide, "Get him out of here. Take him back to his cell and bring that Jack fellow back here too."

When Sten asked him about Solomon, Jack answered, "He's my friend."

"He's right," Solomon said helpfully.

"Look, man, it wasn't me who told them about you. They've been keeping me here illegally because I wouldn't tell them what they wanted to hear."

Frustrated with his excess talking, Sten quickly ordered that Jack be returned to his jail cell. Sten was now convinced that Solomon was the man everyone had been talking about.

"Look, young man, you and I really have some talking to do. The police officer and one of the bank's tellers that were killed during the bank robbery were both my sons. Almost two million dollars were stolen from the bank account cholder's right after the bank's documents went missing. My life has been ruined, and I'm prepared to do whatever it takes to solve this case—it's personal."

Chapter 21

"Now you tell me the truth, and mind my temper—I might shoot you, or even cut your fingers off one by one if I'm made angry. If you tell me everything I want to know, I could work out a good deal and make it easy for you to be a free man very quickly. Now where are the three gentlemen you took from Manhattan in your taxi on the first of April at 11:43 a.m.?" Sten asked.

"I have never seen these men before, and who is Philippe?" Solomon asked.

"He is the police officer who said he saw the robbers getting into your taxi that day and that you were their getaway driver."

"Sir, I don't know what you're talking about," Solomon told him.

"Some people saw you with those gentlemen that day, and they also have shared that information with us. We believe beyond any reasonable doubt that you're keeping the money and the documents for your own selfish interests," Sten shot back, undeterred.

Solomon was shaken when he heard this. "Nobody saw me with any robbers. I'm confused as to why I am here. Why was I arrested, and why am I still being questioned like this? Can't you see that this Philippe is lying? How can a police officer who is investigating a serious robbery see the robbers and let them get away that easily? Are you sure you have the right person"? Solomon asked.

"We have the right person," Sten replied. "If you didn't have anything to do with this and you're not guilty, then why did you flee the country so suspiciously?"

"I wasn't running away from anything. I just wanted a change, so I left the country for a while. I'm an American citizen, and I'm allowed this freedom."

"Look, boy, I know you have the documents and the money, and you know where your other friends are hiding, but the lives of millions of people are at risk here. Don't think we're stupid; we know what you're thinking by keeping them. You could be on death row or looking at life in prison with no chance of parole. Or we work out a deal."

"I want to talk to my lawyer," Solomon insisted.

"You still don't understand the situation. You're in my hands now, and I decide whether you can talk to your lawyer or not. We have a long way to go before that happens," Sten told him. He walked out of the room, whistling a tune as his men escorted Solomon to his cell.

Sten continued on to a meeting that was already in progress.

***

"Now that everyone knows what's going on, I'm open to suggestions about how to progress from here," Sten stated.

One of his officers said, "With the way this man Solomon was answering your questions, it's difficult to know whether Philippe was telling the truth."

"So what should we do?" another officer asked.

"I will torture both of them until somebody tells me the truth. Right now I'm going to concentrate on Philippe because I believe that he might be trying to betray his department. As for Solomon, if we torture him, he will tell us what we want to know. If he doesn't tell us, then I will have to presume that he's innocent, and we will release him," Sten answered.

Everyone agreed, and they decided to proceed at once.

Sten ordered that both Philippe and Solomon be subjected to as much misery as possible.

Later that day Solomon saw massive, muscular men coming toward his cell. They unlocked the cell, went in, and told him to remove all of his clothing. Once he was naked, they led him out of the cell and took him to another cell—this one had no window. There was no mattress or blankets on the silver iron bed, no lights, and no toilet. The bed was made of steel and was painfully cold. They put him in there and showed him a little button; if he needed to go to the toilet or wanted something to eat, he should press it.

Solomon tried to make himself comfortable on the floor and reassure himself that they would release him as soon as they found that he was innocent. He thought about suing them and making them pay millions of dollars for punishing him unjustly.

When Solomon had to urinate, he pressed the red button. Two security guards came and asked him, "What can we do for you, sir?"

"I need to urinate," Solomon told them. He thought they would take him somewhere to use the toilet, but they told him to wait. They returned with a brown rubber bucket. "What do you want me to do with this?" he asked.

"Use it. This is your commode now. When it gets full, you call us to empty it. If you need anything else, press the button."

Solomon shouted, "Are you people crazy? How can you expect me to use this?" But they weren't listening and continued to walk away.

Two hours later, after he had something to eat, he felt like smoking a cigarette, so he pressed the button again.

The guards returned, and Solomon asked them for a cigarette.

"Do you really want to smoke a cigarette?" they asked.

"Badly," Solomon replied.

One of the guards took out a cigarette and lit it. The guard took a long drag and blew the smoke into the air so Solomon could smell it, and then the guard stubbed it out. He put it back in the pack, and the two guards walked away laughing.

Solomon's urge for a smoke was getting intense. He couldn't think straight, and he felt like he was going crazy. Solomon started calling the guards all kinds of names, but they ignored him and kept laughing. He cursed them and their mothers. When the guards heard this, they came back, opened his cell door, and brutally beat the hell out of him. He was left lying on the floor crying.

They wouldn't allow him to take a shower, and he was only allowed three glasses of water a day. He continued to use the bucket to urinate, but the bucket was very big, and it would take at least a week for it to get full. Meanwhile the odor was becoming unbearable, and when the guards came to see him, they wore masks.

After a week in this environment, an officer came to ask Solomon if he was ready to tell them the truth. They too were wearing masks.

Solomon said, "What I told Sten is all I know, and if I said anything different, it would be a lie."

Sten told them to keep at him and increase his punishment. Now he was only allowed two meals a day and three glasses of hot water, but the water had to be drunk within a five-minute time limit, or it would be taken away. They also beat the bottoms of his feet with a piece of plywood; the pain was excruciating.

Since Solomon had made up his mind not to tell them anything, he was willing to accept any punishment they handed out. When the bucket had filled with urine, Solomon decided to push the red button to see if they would empty it. The guards came and saw that it wasn't yet filled to the brim. One of the guards picked it up and threw it all over Solomon, and it splashed on his walls and bed. That was the worst day in Solomon's life, and it provoked an anger that made him ready to kill the guard with his bare hands. The guards didn't seem to care; they slammed his cell door closed and left him like that. They were trying to break his will, but as the days went by, Solomon refused to speak; when they had splashed the urine all over him, he had vowed to stay silent.

When Sten realized that his plans weren't working, he decided he would try something else—he would deal directly with Solomon's mother. He went to Chicago with a couple of his men. When they met with Clare, they told her that they had finally found her son and that he had been questioned and released. Afterward he had traveled back to Europe, and they knew that she was aware of his plans.

"Yes, he did actually call me from there, and I was very happy for him. I hope he can make some good connections with some nice people as he has done in the past. I'm praying for him," Clare told them.

"But ma'am, we have a big problem here," Sten told her.

"What is the problem?" she asked.

"For some reason your son was kidnapped in Sweden by the Hell Angels gang who said he stole some documents and money from them, and we have heard that they're planning to kill him. We've been trying to find out what they want from him, but so far we haven't been successful. We are working with the Swedish authorities to arrange for his release. If there are any further developments, we will let you know," Sten replied.

Chapter 22

When Solomon's mother heard this, she cried. Sten tried to calm her down by telling her that everything was going to be fine and that they were working on a solution that would bring Solomon back safely to the States.

"Please don't cry. Just pray for him," he told her.

Sten went to his hotel to do some thinking. He felt that the case was getting too complicated for him, and the pressures coming from the governor and the mayor's office were too great in New York. He just needed to find out if Solomon's mother knew anything that could help solve the case. He decided to have two of his best agents, Denny Knowing and Martine Bear, who were known for their creative thinking, obtain more information on Solomon and the missing documents by dealing with Solomon's mother.

After speaking with Sten, the two officers came up with the plan to make contact with someone else who had been close to Solomon. When they went through Solomon's file, they came across Jack and noticed that Sten had released him from jail two weeks ago. They decided to fly back to New York to pay him a visit.

***

Back in New York, walking in his neighborhood and minding his business, Jack noticed two FBI agents walking toward him, and stricken with fear over his last encounter with law enforcement, he turned to flee. However, they saw what he was trying to do and chased him down. Jack was fast, but they were faster; and before he knew it, he was on the ground and being handcuffed. They took him back to Chicago to a little motel room they had rented. Denny and Martine took off the handcuffs and removed the tape from his mouth.

"Why did you kidnap me and put the tape across my mouth?" Jack shouted at them.

"Because you wouldn't keep your mouth shut," Denny told him.

"I thought we already went through this in New York. I told you people then that I didn't know anything about anything. Why are you still so interested in me?" Jack asked.

"OK, here's the plan," Martine began. "We want you to convince Solomon's mother Clare that some Hell Angels gang abducted Solomon from his home, and they are threatening to kill him because they think

Solomon is keeping some documents and money he had stolen from them. Tell Clare that she only has a week to come up with the documents and money, or else Solomon will be killed. Tell her you were with him when he was captured, but they let you go so you could tell her the news; instead you went to the Swedish government to ask for their help, and they notified the FBI, which is presently working with the Swedish authorities to save Solomon's life. You later flew back to inform her about the situation.

"Let Clare know that's why we are trying our best to get Solomon released, but we can't do anything more without the money or the documents. We know that if she hears the story from you, she will be more inclined to believe it than if we were to tell her—we've already questioned her about the documents. That's all we really want you to do."

"That's all you want me to do? I hope you guys aren't playing games with me," Jack said.

"No, we aren't, and we might even be able to give you a job working with us. Wouldn't that make you happy? Trust us," Denny told him.

"Look, man. I'm not going to sit here and listen to all these promises. If you're serious about this, then write it down on paper so I'm convinced you really do mean what you're saying. If I'm going to put my life on the line by betraying a good friend, then I need some kind of a guarantee," Jack told them.

"Look, this is a government agency. We believe in trust, and we work in trust, so you're just going to have to take our word for it and believe what we're telling you. This is the way we do things," Martine said.

"Well, I don't think I'm prepared to commit to anything like this with only words as a guarantee. The man is my best friend for Christ's sake. You guys are FBI agents, and you have the power to do anything you want. If I take your word and do this dirty job, and I don't get what I've been promised, who will believe me? With my long criminal record, it will be my word against yours," Jack replied.

The two officers could see that Jack wasn't joking. They told him they needed time to think things over; they would come back later and talk to him again. They called Sten, who arranged for the money they had asked for—they needed to provide Jack with some positive incentives. Jack stayed with them that day, and they made him very comfortable until the following day.

On the following day, Martine asked Jack to walk outside with them, and sitting there was a new Toyota Corolla. Martine handed him the keys to the car along with a gas pass that would provide him with free gas for one year, courtesy of the FBI. In addition there was a check in the amount of two thousand dollars.

Jack was now convinced they had been telling him the truth.

"I haven't seen this much money in a long time," he admitted.

"So do we have a deal?" Denny asked.

"Yes, we have a deal," agreed Jack.

"Great, but this isn't everything. Like we told you yesterday, if you help us, we'll be happy to have you work for us," they told him.

"I'm ready to do anything that you ask me to do," Jack told them.

They told him that he should go out, enjoy himself, find a nice hotel to relax in, and meet with them back at the FBI office the following day. Denny gave him a card with the Chicago office's address on it.

The next day he met with Martine and Denny at their office, and they went over the instructions about what they wanted him to do. They hooked him up to a recording device and handed him a photograph they had doctored showing Solomon in the hands of a group of men. The photo indicated that Solomon had been tortured—there was blood all over his face. The plan was that once Jack had the story down pat, they would drop him off close to Clare's house.

Chapter 23

"Don't act suspiciously, but show some remorse and try to convince her that you're telling her the truth. It's very important that you keep the device in your ear so we can tell you what to say and do," Martine advised.

"Don't worry. I'm sure that when I see her, she'll believe anything I tell her because she has known me for a long time, and she knows I'd never do anything to harm her or her son," Jack told them.

They drove to the planned destination and told Jack to take deep breaths to dispel any lingering fear. They told him they'd be waiting for him and that they had arranged a taxi to take him to Clare's house.

Jack arrived at the house and rang the doorbell. She answered the door and was quite surprised to see Jack. She gave him a big hug and welcomed him into her house. Solomon's mother had one of her neighbors over to visit. Jack tried to act pleasant, but from the look on his face, she knew that there was something terrible he had to say.

"Is this about my son?" she asked.

Jack waited to hear a response from the officers; then he shook his head up and down indicating yes.

Clare quickly turned to her friend. "Please excuse me, but could we postpone our visit for the time being so I can speak to Jack?"

When her friend left, she asked Jack to sit down and brought him a glass of cold water. She sat down and looked directly into his eyes, which were full of fear, and she was certain it was bad news. She became anxious, breathing quickly, and braced herself to hear what Jack had come all the way from New York to tell her.

"Tell me the news," she requested nervously.

Jack took the photo from his pocket and showed it to her. She tried to brace herself for the worst. Slowly and carefully, his voice cracking with nervousness, Jack explained everything to her that Denny and Martine had told him to say. What she was hearing was a repeat of what the two officers had already told her a couple of days ago. She hadn't really taken what they said seriously until she saw the photo Jack had just shown her.

"Did Solomon give you any documents to keep for him?" Jack asked.

Clare paused for a moment while looking in his eyes, and at that instant she decided to carry out what she promised her son and not say anything.

"No, not that I'm aware of," she answered.

"If you know anything about these documents and the money, then you should let me know so we can save your beloved son's life. He's my best friend, and I'm willing to help him any way I can—even if it costs me my life—because he is a good man and doesn't deserve anything like this," said Jack as tears ran from the corner of his eyes.

Clare could see the love that Jack had for her son, but she believed that people would do anything for the sake of money, so she stuck to the story she had told him earlier.

With all of the crying that Jack was doing, something kept telling her not to reveal anything. Once Jack realized he wasn't going to get any more information out of her, he told her they would have to rely on the FBI to do its job. He left her with the photo and gave her his phone number to call him if she found out anything more about the documents. "If you can think of anything else, I may even go to Sweden and try to rescue Solomon and bring him back to the States."

Clare walked outside with him to his waiting taxi. She watched as the taxi left, and then she slowly walked back to the house. She picked up the photo, looked at it, and then she cried. She thought about what Jack had told her and whether he was telling her the truth. She could lose her son over pieces of paper. The guilt settled. If her son died because of these documents and money, God in heaven would hold her responsible.

At that moment they were watching her on the cameras that Newark David and William Frowner had installed. They could see that things were really getting through to her because she couldn't eat or sleep in peace, and every time she looked at the photograph, she would cry again. Her only son, where was he?

***

Meanwhile the odor in Solomon's cell was becoming worse. It was so powerful that he got sick and felt like he was dying. One of the guards relayed the information to Sten, who ordered the cell to be cleaned and Solomon taken to the infirmary. The on-site doctor told the guards that Solomon had a high fever. He prescribed some medicine that he asked the guards to give him with food when he woke up. The guards followed the doctor's orders, but now Sten was scared. He ordered Solomon be moved to a nicer cell with a toilet and that he be given a bed with a mattress and clean sheets. He was to eat as much as he wanted, and Solomon would no longer be tortured.

The guards did as they were told. The only thing missing from Solomon's cell were cigarettes and his freedom. The guards finally brought him a cigarette and allowed him to have a smoke. He thought he was in heaven and enjoyed it from start to finish, but they never brought him another. Instead they stood in front of his cell smoking their cigarettes, allowing the smell to waft in.

A few days later, Sten brought him back to the interrogation room. He asked Solomon, "How are you doing today?"

Solomon replied, "What do you want me to say? Do you want me to tell you that I'm fine? Of course not, I'm dying here."

"Do you have anything you want to tell me now?" Sten asked.

"Like what?" Solomon replied.

"Like telling me the truth about everything that happened during the bank robbery and the people who were involved. I'd like you to cooperate and help us by telling us the truth. That way we can all go back to our nice little lives and put this behind us," Sten told him.

"Sir, why don't you just kill me right now and get it over with because I am sick and tired of seeing your face; it's causing me nightmares," Solomon growled.

"What are you talking about? You haven't answered my question," Sten said.

"What I'm telling you is that you believe I have something you're looking for, and you believe what that man Philippe has told you, so there's no way that you're going to believe anything I tell you. If I had anything at all that belonged to anybody, I would return it to the rightful owner. I might have gone to jail in the past for fraud and theft, but that doesn't mean I'm an evil person. I made a terrible mistake then, and I went to jail and paid the price for getting involved with the wrong people. I don't deserve to be treated this way."

Sten listened carefully and watched Solomon's facial expressions. He was touched but didn't reveal any of his feelings.

"You know, your mother is in our hands, and she is presently in a jail cell undergoing the same type of treatment that you've received. She is experiencing a great deal of pain, and it might even kill her soon," Sten told him.

Solomon suddenly felt sick to his stomach. He didn't want his mother to die for something he believed in. He shook and fell to the ground in tears. "Save my mother, oh God, from the hands of this evil man!"

But Solomon was not prepared to tell him anything. He was only praying that they would believe what he had told them.

"Get him out of here, and take him back to his jail cell!" Sten ordered, and Solomon was roughly carried out.

"Please stop hurting my mother! Leave her alone! We are innocent. Let her go please!" Solomon pleaded as he was tossed back into his cell.

One of Sten's assistants saw what had gone on and told him, "I don't really think Solomon knows anything about this robbery. He has undergone a tremendous amount of torture, and it's been enough to make any man talk. We are concentrating all our energy only on him, and we seem to be forgetting about our own man. Philippe is the only person who had any contact with the people we're looking for, and I think he's capable of selling the information to criminals. What I'm trying to say is that we've worked hard in going through all the evidence we have pertaining to Solomon, and without any further solid proof that he was involved, I would like you to give him the benefit of the doubt."

Chapter 24

Sten turned and looked at his other men, and they too shook their heads in agreement.

"I can't believe you people. How can you want me to give this man with such a criminal history the benefit of the doubt? The governor's office is calling every day and pressuring me to find the responsible party, and you want me to go along with your thinking? No way!"

Solomon was asleep when one of the security guards roughly woke him up and told him to get dressed because he had a visitor. Solomon wondered who it might be. He was escorted to a little room where he saw his good friend Jack. Solomon went over to Jack and hugged him happily.

Jack spoke first. "You know I love you, and I want to help you in any way I can, but these guys are convinced you're in possession of something they're looking for. Your mother is just dying because of what they have you in here for. They've told her they're quite prepared to kill not only you but her as well if you don't give them back what they want."

"Look, man. I don't know where you're coming from or what they did to you, but I really don't know what you're talking about. Do you think I want my mother to die? I don't know why they're doing this to us. I don't know what more you want me to do," Solomon replied.

"What about the documents you told me you had in your possession when they came looking for you and you needed my help to leave the country? Aren't these the same documents? Please, just give them back so we can walk out of here!"

Angry, Solomon cried out, "I thought you were here to help me, not to lie by saying I told you about having some documents! You know we didn't talk about anything like that. Did they pay you to tell these lies, or did you come here to mock me? I don't want to ever see you again."

He stood up and asked the security guard to take him back to his cell. As he was leaving, Jack stood up and said, "I'm trying to help save your life and your mother's life."

When Jack walked into the officers' office, he told them he couldn't help anymore. "I've tried, but the man doesn't seem to know what you're keeping him for."

Denny and Martine flew back to Chicago to implement a fresh plan. As everybody knew each other in Clare's neighborhood, they decided to inform her neighbors that her son, Solomon, was in trouble, and she was the only one who could save him because he had entrusted her with something important that his kidnappers wanted returned. They printed up copies of the original photo they had of Solomon and wrote a note on the bottom asking her neighbors to talk to her so that they might save her son's life. They put a notice in all of the mailboxes belonging to her neighbors.

Later that day, once everyone saw the photograph of Solomon, the community leader called a quick meeting, but Solomon's mother was excluded. He took out the photograph of Solomon and told them that one of their own neighbors had a problem and needed their help—nobody wanted to see Solomon dead. Since the only person who could help him was his own mother, he asked for ideas from the group on what was the best way to convince her to do whatever she could to save her son's life.

One of the residents, Mrs. Brownell, suggested, "We should talk to her and see if these allegations are the truth, and then we might find the best way we can help."

Everyone agreed with her idea; one neighbor who was very close to Solomon's mother suggested they all go to her house at once and talk to her.

"I don't think that's a good idea. I will go with my assistant and Mrs. Brownell to speak to her," the community leader suggested. Everyone was dismissed, and the group went to visit Solomon's mother.

When she opened the door and saw them standing there, Clare welcomed them into her home. The look on her face was not pleasant, and this brought them more concern.

Mr. Stewart Williamson, the community leader, took out Solomon's photograph and held it in his hand. "We know what you're having problems with, and that's why we came here to offer our assistance and find out if we can help."

Clare looked into their faces that radiated with love and concern and knew they were willing to help her. She explained what the FBI officers had told her and what her son's good friend had said. She took out the photograph Jack had brought to her and showed it to them. She became overwhelmed.

Of course the FBI was observing all of this on their cameras.

The community leader and her neighbor showed Clare the notice they had received in their mailboxes. They told her that the entire community knew about the situation, and they were very concerned and wanted to help.

Mr. Stewart asked her, "Did your son give you something to keep for him?" She reiterated what she had told the FBI without changing her story. Mr. Stewart and the others believed her. They told her to contact them if she found out anything else.

Denny and Martine talked as they watched everything that had happened on the camera.

"I really don't think she knows what's going on. I think we should end this; we're just killing her, and it isn't helping our investigation," Denny told Martine.

"I agree," said Martine.

When Sten heard the news from Chicago, he thought that perhaps he should hold Philippe more responsible for the disappearance of the documents and release Solomon. He, too, was starting to believe that Solomon was innocent.

Clare went to her parents' home as she was wholly distressed from the day's events and did not want to be alone. However, unable to sleep that night, Clare decided she would go home to remove the documents from the hole under her bed and return them to the FBI. She would not give them to any of the officers she had dealt with; she would take them to Sten himself.

However, a few hours later, she changed her mind and got up to think about what to do next. She kissed her parents and said good-bye to them and that she would see them again soon. Clare got into her car and drove back home. By this time the FBI agents had already finished removing the cameras and microphones from her house.

On her return Clare sat down to think. She called her cousin Lemont Jensen who came and helped her dig out the bag from among her flower garden. Lemont didn't ask any questions and just did as she told him.

He was actually excited that he was able to help Clare out. She didn't ask him to clean up because it was late at night, and Lemont wanted to get some sleep and get prepared for work the next day. Clare thanked him profoundly and sent him home.

Then she made copies of the documents in her little basement office; the photocopies were put into another bag and carefully wrap in four black garbage bags and hid in the original location. Clare then slowly dug a hole in the soft dirt just a little distant from the original hole in her backyard garden, placed the bag of documents in four black Garbage bags, and put it into the hole, which she disguised with some planted flowers.

Afterward she purchased a ticket for Stockholm, Sweden, and would leave that same week. This would allow her to quickly prepare her travel documents and the other necessary papers she would need for her journey. Clare secretly traveled to Stockholm that week and left her house and her two German shepherds in the care of Mrs. Brownell.

Chapter 25

After much thinking, Sten decided to have Clare killed before something else happened.

The following day Mrs. Brownell, who was taking care of Clare's dogs, came with the dogs to check on Clare's house. While inside, an explosion blew Mrs. Brownell and the two German shepherds to smithereens. Nobody knew that Sten had this carried out.

Clare's neighbors were terrified at the belief that Clare had perished in the bombing. Everyone ran out of their homes, afraid that they might be blown up too. The streets were crowded with people, and thick black smoke rose into the air. The Chicago police were trying hard to hold back the crowds while the people who had arrived first were searching among the rubble for any possible survivors.

Once the police had everything under control and the flames were out, they looked for the cause of the explosion. They knew this was not a normal situation and that such a fate shouldn't happen to such a good woman. Soon the FBI team from Chicago took over the investigation. The local Chicago TV stations treated it as breaking news, and later that day all of the other television stations across the United States were reporting on the bombing and showing photographs of Solomon's mother, saying that she was the only fatality.

Some remains were found in the rubble, and the FBI arranged for DNA testing to determine that some of the remains were in fact human. The remains were taken to the hospital, where Clare's family was able to make funeral arrangements.

When Mr. Carter's morning newspaper was delivered, he took it into the kitchen to read, and the front-page headlines stunned him. He quickly read the news and pretended he couldn't believe what he was reading or seeing. Leaving his breakfast on the table, he went to his bedroom and showed the paper to his wife.

"I'll read it later—just put it on the table. I'm watching a program on television right now," she told him.

"No, dear, you have to read it now. It's very important that you read it," he insisted.

"Sorry, dear, but I am busy right now," she said.

Mr. Carter walked over and turned off the television. Mrs. Carter started screaming at her husband.

"Calm down, calm down! I know this program is very important to you, but a member of our family has been blown up, and it's front-page news. That's why I want you to read it right away," he told his wife.

She angrily grabbed the paper from him and looked at the headlines. As she read the story, she cried. Without delay Mr. Carter called the airline and booked a ticket to Chicago.

"Honey, I want you to stay here and look after little Derrick and the business."

"Where are you going?" his wife asked.

"I'm going to Chicago."

"OK, but please call me as soon as you get there," she requested.

"You know I will; I always do. I'll be picking my ticket up at the airport in a couple of hours."

The doorbell rang.

"I just called a taxi, and it's already here," he told his wife. He picked up his bag and went to the door. Standing on his doorstep was a man he had never seen before.

"Are you the taxi driver?" he asked.

"No, sir. I came to see you because I believe I might have some information about the woman that was killed by the bomb in Chicago."

"What is your name?" Mr. Carter asked.

"My name is Jack Epstein. Clare's son, Solomon, was a very good friend of mine. We lived in the same community, and we grew up together in Chicago. I, too, was arrested and questioned about an incident involving Solomon when they were searching for him."

Mr. Carter was a little confused. "But why did you come to see me? How did you know that I knew these people?" he asked Jack.

"I came here once to drop off Solomon, and Solomon told me a lot of good things about you that day. Also Clare used to say nice things about you too."

"So you do know something about me after all. Look, I'm on my way to Chicago. I don't know whether you have heard about it, but it's all over the front page of *The New York Times*. I'm going to find out what happened. If there's any way I can help bring this killer to justice, I will," Mr. Carter told him.

"Yes, I saw it on the news last night, and it got me thinking about how I might be able to help. That's when I remembered you, so I came here to talk to you, but you already know all about it. By the way Solomon was arrested. I was only able to see him once," Jack told him.

While they were talking, Mr. Carter's taxi arrived. He handed Jack some money and told him to buy a ticket to Chicago on the next flight—they could talk more there. Jack took the money and asked him for a phone number.

Mr. Carter flew to Chicago and went directly to the lot where Clare's house used to stand. The once charming house had been reduced to a pile of ashes. The tragic sight brought Mr. Carter to tears. But the police wouldn't allow him to stay in the area. He asked to speak to the officer in charge of the investigation.

"Why? Do you have information that might assist us with our investigation?" the officer asked him.

Mr. Carter told him all that he knew about Clare and her family. When he finished the officer gave him the information he had requested.

He took a taxi and went to rent himself a car. He called his wife to let her know what he had found, and she cried. He had no sooner hung up the phone when it rang again. It was Jack.

"I'm at the airport. Could you come and get me?" he asked.

"OK, just stand outside," Mr. Carter said.

After Mr. Carter picked up Jack, they went to a restaurant and ordered some drinks.

"Now tell me everything that you know. I saw the house, and it was surreal, but the reality is that it really did happen," Mr. Carter said to him.

Jack took his time and told Mr. Carter everything he knew, from how he had originally helped Solomon out of the country to how he was forced to work on behalf of the FBI to try to save Solomon's life.

Mr. Carter suddenly asked him, "How do I know you don't have any wires on you or that you're not still working for them?"

Jack unbuttoned his shirt to show he was being truthful. "Just last night I was shot at twice when I was coming back from the beer store, and I only just escaped with my life. I guess they want to kill me too. I haven't even gone back to my house since it happened."

"But why would they want to kill you? Who do you think wants to kill you?" Mr. Carter asked.

"The FBI—they think I know too much. When I was forced to work for them, they told me a lot of stuff pertaining to their case. You're going to have to trust me. Sten's two sons were killed in that robbery, and he is ready to take his anger out on anybody he thinks might know something about their deaths," Jack told him.

"How do I know it wasn't you who told them evil things about this lovely family and that is what has caused all their troubles today? You sit here and ask me to trust you? Well, let me tell you straight out right now that I only trust God first, and after that only my mother. I'm sorry for making you come to Chicago. I know that you were Solomon's best friend, but you sold him out to the FBI as well. Take this money." He handed Jack a thousand dollars. "Stay the hell away from me. I don't want to know you or ever see you again."

Chapter 26

Mr. Carter angrily stormed out of the restaurant. He got in his car and drove to the offices of the Chicago FBI. The FBI welcomed Mr. Carter, and he told them everything that had happened to Solomon's family in New York: how they had arrested Solomon, tortured him, and kept him in their jail with no evidence to support his arrest. He also told them that he planned to offer a reward of thirty thousand dollars to anyone who came forward and provided information that might lead to the arrest of the person or persons responsible for the terrible murder of Solomon's mother.

The FBI made the necessary arrangements for announcing to the public his offer of a reward. Not long after, a woman who claimed to be a very good friend of Clare's called. She said she had seen two men hanging around the house the day before the bombing. She was quite prepared to meet with the FBI and give a description of the individuals. The composite sketch the FBI prepared was run through the FBI database, but no match was found.

In the meantime, after spending a few days with Clare's family, Mr. Carter returned to New York. He informed his wife of everything that had happened in his absence. He found out that Jack had been murdered. Now he finally believed the story that Jack had tried to tell him when they had talked in the restaurant.

After what had happened, Mr. Carter was afraid they might come after him and his family as well, but he was also trying to think of ways to get Solomon out of the hands of Sten. His wife suggested he contact his lawyer and seek his help.

They were about to get another big-time lawyer from Brooklyn by the name of Liquor Johnson. Johnson told him not to worry about anything; he would arrange for Solomon's freedom and make sure no further harm came to him. Mr. Carter felt reassured about his abilities to have Solomon released. Johnson also suggested that he hire bodyguards—just as a precaution. Mr. Carter took his advice and obtained the services of a security service to protect him and his family.

Philippe and his family were freed because Sten now believed his story, but he was suspended from the NYPD without pay until the situation calmed down.

One day Solomon was sitting solemnly in his cell when he received a visitor. It was Sten. He sat down and looked at Solomon.

"You know mothers are the greatest people in the world. They love their children so much, and they would do anything they could to save their children's lives. Your mother, Clare, must love you very much. We've decided to let you go." Sten smiled at him. "I would like you to tell me some things about Clare, your mother who made you believe you could trust her."

Solomon laughed. "My mother is the greatest person I have ever known. I remember how sweet she always was. When I was a little boy, whenever she prepared food and brought it to me, if I didn't eat, she wouldn't eat. When it was time to go to bed, she'd keep coming into my room to make sure I was comfortable enough, and if I couldn't sleep, she wouldn't sleep. Whenever I got sick, she would take me to the hospital and fast and pray to God to make me well again.

"She always wanted me to be the best son in the world. She was so proud to have me as her son, and she always looked at the good side of me and ignored the bad. Every time I looked in her eyes, I could see how much she loved me, and I was protected because of her love. She always thought about me before she thought of herself. She always advised me to do the right thing. Sometimes I thought she was being hard on me, but now I realize she was giving me a lot of precious advice for my own good," Solomon told him with tears running down his face.

"But what do you want to do with these documents?" Sten asked.

"I don't know what the hell you're talking about!" Solomon shouted. "I don't deserve this treatment!"

"This mistake has led to your mother's death." He took out the newspaper and showed Solomon the headlines.

Solomon took the paper and, with trembling hands, took in the news. He threw the paper to the ground and stepped on it, screaming, "No! No! What happened?" He picked up the newspaper and read it to make sure what he was reading was true. Sten looked at Solomon and told him that he was the person who had arranged to have her killed. They knew she was in possession of the documents, and anyone who wasn't authorized to have any knowledge of them had to die; the information could not be made public.

"In addition," Sten said, "your friend Jack is also dead," and he showed him a photograph of Jack's body.

"We now have your uncle and his family on our hit list. It's only a matter of time before he is killed because he can't keep his mouth shut. Once we've eliminated everyone on our list, then I will slit your throat and kill you myself. It's too bad that things turned out this way. After today don't be too surprised when some changes occur around here.

"We got the three robbers with some help from a tip after their pictures appeared on the America's Most Wanted website. They confessed the truth and told us that you have all the documents and the money, and I believe them." He got up and left Solomon screaming and swearing at him.

"My relatives didn't do anything to you. If you think it was my fault, then just kill me! No more innocents need to succumb to your evil plans and be killed!" Solomon yelled.

Sten stopped suddenly and turned around with a smile on his face. "No, those men that I want to kill are not innocent. They put their noses into something that didn't concern them. As for you it won't be necessary to worry about dying because I plan to kill you soon. You'll be able to eat well, drink well, and sleep well because I want you to be healthy when I finally do kill you. You need to feel the pain and know how badly I hate you.'

He walked away laughing.

Chapter 27

Mr. Carter's lawyer, Johnson, sent a letter to Sten demanding that Solomon be released at once—unless he had definite charges, which should be handled through the appropriate court channels. Johnson was prepared to take the matter to the Supreme Court if necessary. Sten knew Mr. Johnson to be one of the most powerful and respected attorneys in the United States. Nevertheless, he didn't bother to respond to Johnson's multiple letters and faxes.

With the lack of cooperation from Sten, he decided he had no choice but to take the matter to court. Solomon needed to be charged or released.

Bodyguards now surrounded Mr. Carter and his family day and night, although this hadn't prevented several attempts to shoot him. All he wanted at this point was for Solomon to be free.

The FBI was unable to accumulate enough evidence to indict Sten and his department for the murder of Solomon's mother until Mr. Carter remembered the story that Jack had told him about the two FBI agents he had worked with. Mr. Carter provided the FBI with the agents' names. After the two men were questioned, the FBI placed it entire office in New York under investigation.

Sten's office was under mounting pressure from the Chicago FBI office's investigation of the murder of Solomon's mother. The evidence against Solomon submitted to the court was not strong enough to send him to trial, so the court demanded that Solomon be released. In the event that Sten obtained more evidence against him, they were to submit it to a judge so an arrest warrant could be issued.

Bowing to the pressure, Sten had no choice but to release Solomon. However, he planned to hire a professional to kill him as soon as possible.

On the day of Solomon's release, Mr. Carter arrived with his bodyguards to pick him up.

"I will make sure you don't leave my sight. You're my son now," Mr. Carter told him.

A room had been prepared for him back at Mr. Carter's home. Solomon took a long, hot shower and changed into some clean clothes. When he and Mr. Carter finally sat down to talk, Solomon couldn't stop crying and talking about his mother's death. Solomon told Mr. Carter what Sten had said to him about his mother and Jack's death. Mr. Carter told him they wouldn't be able to use the conversation against Sten because it gave no substantial proof; they were only words. It took him a while to calm Solomon down.

After supper Mr. Carter went down to the basement and brought out a box, which he handed to Solomon.

"What is this?" he asked.

"Open it," Mr. Carter said.

Solomon opened it and saw a large sum of money.

"Why are you giving me this?" Solomon asked.

"I'm not giving it to you. It's yours. You gave it to me for safekeeping long before you went to jail; don't you remember?" he asked.

"Oh my God! I forgot about this. Thank you very much. I always knew I could trust you. Thanks again," Solomon said.

A month after Solomon's release, Sten and his family were killed in a plane crash on their way to a family reunion in Baltimore, Maryland. This allowed the FBI to pursue the bank robbing case with less fanaticism and more legality. However, Sten had already paid someone to do his dirty work, and an officer was presently on the hunt for Solomon, despite Sten's death.

With all the troubles falling on Solomon, he was advised by the Carter family to leave the country and to stay away until everything had settled down. Their destination of choice was Sao Paulo, Brazil. The necessary documents were obtained. Solomon deposited money into a new bank account. His children came to spend the day with him before he departed and accompanied him to the airport. Unfortunately the hit man Sten hired was closing in and traveling on the same plane. When Solomon landed in Brazil, he arranged for a hotel room, but little did he know that the hit man had taken a room next to his.

That night the hit man bought a gun from a local gang in the east end of Sao Paulo. He put a silencer on it. He placed it carefully in his pocket and left his room. He walked directly to Solomon's door and knocked. Thinking it might be room service, Solomon opened the door, and the hit man opened fire. He shot Solomon three times and quickly walked away, leaving Solomon bleeding profusely on the floor and calling out for help.

An older man and his wife who were just leaving their room heard his cries. They rushed over and found Solomon slumped on the floor, covered in blood. The old man stayed with Solomon and tried to help him while his wife ran back to her room to call for help. An ambulance was called, and he was taken to the hospital. The doctors doubted he would pull through, but after several surgeries to repair a damaged left leg and left shoulder, he survived. However, he spent almost two weeks in the hospital recovering from his injuries. He didn't let Mr. Carter or his children know about what had happened.

The Brazilian police told him they had searched high and low for the man who had shot him, but it appeared that he had been long gone before they arrived. The hit man knew that Solomon wasn't dead, and while he was in the hospital recovering, the hit man made several unsuccessful attempts to finish the job. He decided to stay in Sao Paulo and wait until Solomon was discharged from the hospital before he made any further attempts. Next time he would shoot him in the head to make sure he'd be finished off.

Solomon had been in contact with his friends and family in the States, and he let them think he was fine and that everything was going well with him. Solomon was feeling good and decided to stop at a nearby bar. He sat and watched men play pool for money. One of the men lost all of his money and walked over to where Solomon was sitting. He took out a gun, which he set down in front of Solomon. The man asked him if he was interested in buying it. Solomon picked up the gun, checked it over, and saw that it was a .45 automatic pistol. The man wanted to sell it because he needed more money to continue betting—he'd lost almost two thousand dollars.

"Is this gun clean?" Solomon asked.

"Oh yes, it's very clean. I have never had any occasion to use it," he replied.

Solomon bought the gun from him; he knew it was hard to find. He put it in his pocket and returned to his hotel.

He carried the gun on him everywhere he went. Three weeks after searching, Solomon finally secured a downtown apartment and found a job working at a gas station. He was tired of just sitting around and doing nothing. Shortly after he started his new job, the hit man found out where Solomon was staying. When he thought the time was right, he entered Solomon's apartment building, walked up to Solomon's door, and knocked. Solomon looked through the peephole and immediately recognized the man who had tried to kill him. Without answering the door, Solomon grabbed his gun and climbed out of his window, making his way to the front door of his building. He slowly walked toward his apartment and hid behind the wall as he watched the hit man trying to break into his apartment.

Solomon quietly went back downstairs and called the police from the hall phone; he told them that someone was trying to break into his apartment to kill him and the man would probably be waiting inside his apartment for him. The Brazilian police quickly responded to his call. Solomon stood across the street and watched as they arrived. They entered his apartment building, and when they got to his door, they saw that it was open. One of the officers called out in Portuguese, "Is somebody inside here?" As they entered, the gunman shot one of them in the head, killing him instantly. The other officer started shooting at the hit man as he tried to jump out the window. The shot grazed the hit man's head; he stumbled and fell from the window to his death.

Chapter 28

The police took Solomon in for questioning because they wanted to know why this man was trying to kill him. Solomon told them he didn't know why. They finally seemed to believe his story and released him. They also suggested he go to the Brazilian immigration office to renew his visitor's visa if he planned to extend his stay in Brazil. He took their advice and went the following day.

For five years Solomon remained in Brazil. The Carter family and his children came to visit him every year. He finally moved back to New York to be closer to his children and the people who loved him. Mr. Carter and his family were so happy to receive him into their home.

"Come and let me show you something," said Mr. Carter.

He was taken into a big beautiful room, which Mr. Carter had furnished for his very important guests.

"This room has been prepared for you," Mr. Carter told him.

Solomon's mouth fell open as he walked around, gazing at everything and running his hands over the room's objects.

"This is beautiful. I love this room. Thank you very much for letting me stay here in your house. I really appreciate it," Solomon told him.

"You're welcome to stay here as long as you want, and if the time comes when you decide to move into your own place, then you'll take this furniture. I'm giving it all to you," Mr. Carter said. He put his hand into his pocket and took out a check. He handed it to Solomon.

"What's this?" Solomon asked.

"This is money that my wife and I agreed to give you because we know that you don't have very much right now," Mr. Carter said.

"Thank you, sir. I really don't know what to say."

Solomon looked at the amount of the check and exclaimed, "Oh my God! This is too much money. I'm sorry, but I can't accept this. I can only accept your hospitality. I'm sorry."

"You have to take it. We even thought about giving you double, but my wife thought that you might refuse it—just as you're doing now. Please take it, or my wife will be crushed. We're not trying to insult you," Mr. Carter said.

Solomon looked in Mr. Carter's eyes and accepted the check. He gave him a big hug to show his appreciation.

Solomon also called his grandparents, whom he hadn't spoken with for a long time, and reconnected. Hearing their voices again was bittersweet, as they all lamented Clare's death and the hole it left in their hearts. Then he went to look out his bedroom window and noticed Mr. Carter in the garden with little Derrick. He went outside to see them, lifting little Derrick up in his arms and playing with him.

"I was wondering about your son's name," Solomon said.

"Why are you wondering about his name?" Mr. Carter replied.

"Why did you name him Derrick?" asked Solomon. He looked in Mr. Carter's eyes and noticed that something wasn't right. "What's wrong, sir?"

"Nothing. Why do you ask?" Mr. Carter said.

"The funny look on your face when I asked about your son's name," said Solomon.

Mr. Carter sat down in a nearby chair and stared at Solomon. He told his son to go into the house and see his mother. Little Derrick said, "But, Dad, I want to stay here and play with Solomon."

"No, son, you can play with him later. Right now I need to talk to him."

Derrick walked back into the house.

"Sit down, son," Mr. Carter said and took a deep breath before proceeding. "Little Derrick is not my biological son."

"What are you talking about? I don't understand."

"I'm saying he's not my son," Mr. Carter answered.

"Then whose son is he?" Solomon asked.

"He's your blood brother."

"I don't understand what you're saying," Solomon said.

"I'm saying he's your father's son! That's why he is your blood brother. Do you understand me now?" Mr. Carter said as he stood up and put his hands on his waist.

"But how could this happen? My father was your butler. Why would he do something terrible like this to someone like you when you were always so kind to him?" Solomon asked with concern.

Mr. Carter looked at him and sat back down. He put his arm around Solomon's shoulder.

"It wasn't your father's fault. It all happened when I developed a very serious problem with my wife. The only solution I could come up with to fix the problem and keep the woman that I loved was for your father to sleep with my wife.

"Look, I'm sorry for telling you this, but I believe that you're now old enough to understand, and I don't want to hide anything from you anymore," Mr. Carter added.

"Oh my God! Are you telling me that my father cheated on my mother? I can't believe it. My mother was so committed to him," said Solomon.

"No, son, your father did it to save my life; I was ready to kill myself and my wife because I had lost all hope. Your father saved both of our lives, and I'm very grateful to him. I still owe him and would do anything to pay him back because he was a good man," Mr. Carter said.

"How did all this get started? I want to know the whole story," Solomon requested.

"Sorry Solomon, this isn't the right time for this. I will explain everything you want to know later, but first I want you to relax and make yourself comfortable as you think about your future now," Mr. Carter replied.

"I will be traveling to Chicago tomorrow to see my grandparents," Solomon said.

"I will accompany you because I've always wanted to see them again. Your mother, Clare, and I visited them twice, and we had great time," Mr. Carter said.

Chapter 29

When Mr. Carter and Solomon arrived in Chicago, they found Solomon's grandparents outside, cleaning up the yard. My Carter parked the car and they went to greet the elderly couple, who were very excited to see them. After hugging them, Solomon and Mr. Carter helped finish the yard word.

"Why are you doing this yourself? You know full well that Grandpa has already had a heart attack, and I told you guys that I would be coming to visit you," Solomon said to his grandmother.

"It wasn't my idea. He insisted that the yard was dirty, and he wanted to clean things up. I begged him not to do it and told him that I would find someone, especially since the doctor told him not to do anything too physical."

Solomon turned to look at his grandfather, who nodded in agreement. "Yes, that's what happened. You know I hate dirt, especially around my house," he told Solomon.

"But Grandpa, it's very dangerous to ignore the doctor's orders. This is your life we're talking about; you can't do this kind of work," Solomon said.

When they finished tidying up the yard, they all went into the house.

"Wow, this is really a beautiful house," Mr. Carter said.

"Is this your first time here?" Solomon's grandmother asked.

"Yes, ma'am."

They all sat down. Mr. Carter started looking around the living room. A moment later he said, "This living room looks a little dirty. We'll have to get to work and clean it up."

Solomon's grandmother stared at him. "Who do you think you are? You come into my house and start telling me that my house looks dirty. Look, young man, this is our house, and we like it this way. I don't even know you that well; I've only met you a few times when you came here with my daughter, and I never liked you then."

"Grandma, you can't talk to Mr. Carter this way. He's been very kind to us," Solomon told her.

Grandpa spoke up. "Yes, don't talk to him like that. My daughter told me a lot of good things about this man, and from what I've heard, I'll not sit here and let you speak to him like that."

Mr. Carter wanted to diffuse the situation. "You're right. You don't have to like me, and I don't really care about that; but I want you to know that I became part of this family a long time ago, so I have the right to help you stay healthy and happy. I want your old age to be long and comfortable."

"And who gave you that right, Mister?" she asked.

"Well, your granddaughter gives me that right and even your grandson Solomon. You can order me to leave your house right now; I'll leave, and you'll never see me again," Mr. Carter said with a smile.

"No, sir, you can't do that. Can't you see that she's just getting old, and we have to love them?" Solomon said.

Grandma spoke with a gleam in her eye. "Don't take me so seriously. I was only playing with you to see how far I could get before you got angry. I'm sorry for talking to you like that. I heard a lot of good things about you from my late daughter, and I wouldn't talk bad to a man who cares so deeply about us," she told Mr. Carter.

"She's right, son, but please just leave my toaster where it sits. I really love it there," the old man said.

Mr. Carter looked at the two of them and smiled. He took off his jacket, rolled up his sleeves, and said, "Let's get to work!" Solomon rolled up his sleeves as well.

"Wow! Look at those muscles. What did you do to get such big muscles? Have you been taking those bodybuilding supplements to make your muscles grow? Don't you know those things can lead to high blood pressure and heart attacks?" his grandmother said, staring at him.

"No, Grandma, I'm not. I just did lots of training in Brazil. I used to visit the gym five times a week. I didn't realize how well my muscles have developed. I used to see women staring at me when I walked down the street in my T-shirt, but I never realized how handsome I'd become until Mr. Carter told me to take a good look at myself in the mirror the week I returned from Brazil. I think I inherited my father's looks," Solomon told her.

They cleaned the entire house. Later Solomon's grandparents sat him down to have a serious chat.

"I wanted to talk to you about your plans for your future. As my grandson, I love you, and I'm wondering what life will be like for you when we're both gone," his grandmother said.

Solomon looked at them and asked, "Is this what you guys wanted me to come all the way to Chicago for?"

"Yes, son," his grandfather replied.

"I can't believe you people!" Solomon retorted.

"As you can see, I am sick and probably dying. I would like to know what my grandson is going to do with the rest of his life. We both love you so much and care about what will happen to you," his grandfather told him.

"You have to tell them something, Solomon—the truth," Mr. Carter suggested.

"I don't know what I'm going to do with my future. I'm confused. I haven't really sat down and thought about it yet. I've been worrying about Mom. I miss her every day, even more than my father," Solomon confessed.

Mr. Carter stared at them for a moment before saying, "Why don't Solomon and I go back to New York, and you give him some time to think about things. Then he can let you know his decision in a few days. I'll make sure he does the right things this time. Trust me."

Without saying anything, Solomon's grandmother stood up and walked toward the stairs.

"I'm sorry, I don't know what I'm going to do with my future. You can't just walk away from me like that, Grandma," Solomon said.

She stopped and turned to look at him before continuing upstairs.

"So what are we going to do now? Our visit here has turned into a complete nightmare," Solomon told Mr. Carter.

"Let's just sit right here and wait," he replied.

While they were sitting and wondering how they were going to please the old folks, his grandmother came back downstairs carrying a bag. She set it down in front of him and sat down. She looked at Solomon.

"You're right. I'm happy you told us the truth. The reason we wanted you to come see us is that your mother left some things with us to give to you. She asked us to keep them. They looked this way when she originally brought them to us. This is the key to unlock the bag," his grandmother said and handed the keys to Solomon. "You can open it yourself. I'm sure you'll be happy when you see what's inside, just as she thought."

Chapter 30

Solomon quickly opened the bag. The first letter he took out contained a few short words. It read:

> Dear Son,
> You know I love you. You mean everything in the world to me, and I can't stop thinking about you. I can remember when you were a baby, and I was changing your diapers and hearing your voice every time you laughed. When the FBI came to question me about you, I knew things could turn out badly, so I took out a life insurance policy worth half a million dollars and put your name as the beneficiary. I also insured the house and put you on as my beneficiary. It's worth three hundred and seventy-five thousand dollars. I don't know what tomorrow will bring, but just in case anything bad happens, I want you to remember that I love you. Be good to Mr. Carter, and do whatever he tells you to because he loves you also. Please take care of your grandparents. I kept whatever you asked me to keep for you, and no one knows about it. I know you trusted me, and I took that trust very seriously and kept my word. I love you, and I always will.
> Your mother

When he finished reading the letter, Solomon cried. It was almost as if he could hear his mother's voice lifting off the words on the page.

"She wrote this letter like she knew she was going to die," Solomon told them.

"You're a lucky man," Mr. Carter told him.

"Look and see what other things are inside the bag," his grandmother said.

Solomon looked through everything. Most of it was personal items belonging to his mother and father—things that had been very important to them and which she wanted him to keep safe in case anything happened to her.

"My God! It's been five years since my mother died. How can I claim this life insurance money?" Solomon asked.

"I think we should take some time to think about what to do before approaching the insurance company. Put all the documents together so we can take them when we go see a lawyer," Mr. Carter suggested.

"I want to thank you guys so much for this. I'll make sure we do this together. I don't want to live in New York anymore, so I'll probably move here to Chicago to stay closer to you and help take care of you. You know I'm not good with words, but I want you guys to thank Mr. Carter for taking such good care of me.

"I think we'll be returning to New York to work on this stuff, but we'll be in touch with you every day. In the meantime please take care of Grandpa until I can come back."

"Oh I forgot! Wait!" His grandmother went to her room and returned with an envelope. "What's this?" Solomon asked.

"Your mother also left this with us to give to you. Open it up and see what's inside," his grandmother told him.

Inside his mother had written down her bank account number and listed Solomon as her next of kin. She had also written that her son had authorization to claim any money in her account if anything happened to her. Her bank balance was $237,473. Solomon was staggered by the sheer amount of cash. He unlocked the bag with the key and placed the letter inside before relocking it.

He turned to his grandmother and asked, "Is that everything that my mother asked you to give me?"

"Wait, let me think," she replied. "Yes, I think that is all."

"I have an envelope, which your mother gave me before she traveled to New York. I have it right here. I was just waiting for my wife to finish with you first," his grandfather said.

"I love you people; you're just full of surprises," Solomon said with a laugh as he took the envelope. When he opened it up, it contained the deed to the land on which Clare's house had been built, along with all the other documents pertaining to the house.

"OK," Solomon said. "I want you to keep this document here because it's very important to me. I just might build on this land when I come back here to stay for good."

"No problem, son," his grandfather said as he took the envelope and carried it back up to his room. When he came back down, they had some further conversation, and then Solomon and Mr. Carter said their goodbyes. They carried their suitcases out to the car and drove to the airport for their return flight to New York.

At Mr. Carter's house, Solomon arranged all of the documentation; then Mr. Carter took him to see his lawyer friend, so Solomon could finally collect the life insurance funds and claim the money in Clare's bank account.

Solomon flew back to Chicago. He received a check for the half million dollars as well as the other money. He was now a rich man. He gave some money to his grandparents and attempted to give some back to Mr. Carter and his family, but, always generous, they refused. They told him to keep it in his account and not touch it until he thought further about what he wanted to do with it in the future.

He kept his money in the bank and flew back to New York to visit his children. When his ex-wife saw him, she fell in love with him all over again, but Solomon only cared about seeing his children. He relished his time with them while he thought about what to do with his money.

Those days Mr. Carter wasn't spending as much time with Solomon because his business was taking him all over the United States, so he had all the time in the world to think.

He flew to Chicago and built a beautiful house on the land his mother had deeded to him. But before Solomon did build, he went to the land one night and began searching to see if he could find the money and the documents that he had hidden under his mother's flowers garden many years back. He luckily found the bag, but there was no money inside. He thought his mother might have hidden it separately, afraid of losing them both. Only the photocopied documents were neatly stacked inside the bag. These were the documents the FBI almost killed him for. He neatly placed them back in the bag and kept it in his car. He started thinking about what to do with it later. The following day, after much thinking, he decided to burn them that very night so he could erase the memories of the loss they had caused him.

Solomon arranged to move his grandparents into the house with him so he could keep his eye on them and help take care of them.

Six months after moving into his new house, he looked around his new neighborhood and noticed there were no supermarkets nearby, so he bought land six blocks from his house and built a big, beautiful supermarket. His neighbors were thrilled at the much-needed addition.

Solomon employed many of the people from his neighborhood, but he made sure that he was the one running it.

During this time his ex-wife, Mary, started having some tough times with her parents' business. They passed away in a plane crash when they were flying back from England, and though the problems had started long before they died, they escalated afterward.

A very rich man by the name of Watkins McDonald, a prolific, self-made real estate tycoon, decided that the land on which the head office of her parents' business stood would be a perfect location for his son to develop after he graduated from Harvard University. When Mary's parents started having difficulties with their business and were about to declare bankruptcy, they turned to people they felt could help them with a loan—Watkins was one of them. They needed money, and he thought this was the perfect opportunity to acquire their building. He approached them with a plan to give them double the amount of money they needed to get out of bankruptcy, but Mary's parents grew furious and threw him out of their building, telling him never to come around them again.

Watkins in turn got angry and wanted to show them what all his money could do to bankrupt people like them. Meanwhile they had finally been able to get some funds from their friends. They were able to save the company, and they worked hard to build it back up.

But Watkins, who had a reputation for spitefulness, wanted to get back at them badly. He wanted to take revenge for the way they had treated him when he made his original offer to them.

Chapter 31

Watkins felt that he could easily take out his revenge on their daughter. He paid people to follow her and watch her every move, and they in turn came back to him with the information he wanted to know about her. They told Watkins about the people they had seen her with, but he decided to find out who she was in love with by getting close to her. However, Mary's parents had already warned her about Watkins and told her everything that had happened between them.

Over the years things changed. The business was going smoothly, and everyone seemed to have forgotten the past and moved on; but Watkins remained fixated on the incident, and he let his grudge grow and grow like a cancer. He was able to get closer to Mary, and they started seeing a lot of each other. Watkins thought he would like to sleep with her, so he bought her an expensive Rolex watch as a gift and told her how rich and fantastic he was. One afternoon he invited her to dinner at the Sheraton Hotel restaurant, where he had a room all set up. Mary thought it was just a friendly dinner to settle things from their past and discuss other business opportunities.

After dinner, while they were sitting in the hotel lobby and talking, the conversation led to subjects that were more intimate.

"Please tell me everything about yourself. I want to know more about your personal life. Are you married?" Watkins asked.

"I am divorced, but I do have a boyfriend," she replied.

"Is he good to you? Does he treat you well?" he asked.

"Oh yes, he treats me very well. I sometimes think I should have married him instead of my ex-husband. I love him because he treats me like a real woman," Mary said.

"Wow, that's great," he replied. He suggested they go to the bar for a drink. While they were there, he started touching her in a sexual manner. When he tried to kiss her, she became angry and slapped him. "I thought you were trying to be nice to me, but you're trying to seduce me! Well, I have news for you; don't ever come around me again, or I swear I'll kill you." She angrily picked up her purse and walked out on him.

Watkins was left standing alone and laughing. He looked around and tried to tell everyone who saw what happened that she was just playing because she was jealous. After paying for the drinks, he and his men left. In reality he was so angry he could hardly contain himself. Now he really wanted to meet her boyfriend, so he tried to set up a meeting to discuss business with him. He sent his man on Friday to meet with Deon, the man who was in love with Mary and her children. Deon treated them as though they were his own, and he wanted to marry Mary.

The arrangements were made, and Deon came to meet with Watkins. He was welcomed, and everyone in the office appeared happy to see him.

"The reason I asked to see you today is to make you an offer that will make you rich. I'll tell you straight out and not waste your time. I want you to give me all the information you have on your girlfriend Mary's company, such as the company bank account number and other significant information. I'll pay you well if you provide me with the information I'm asking for," Watkins told him.

"But how could you possibly expect me to do this? She's my fiancée, and I love her. She trusts me and I trust her. She pays me very well to be her secretary and treats me with love. I also love her children. Why do you want me to do this for you? You've never seen me before, and you don't know me. Why do you want this information?" Deon asked.

"You're a very handsome young man, and I believe you deserve a good life—not to be sitting in the shadow of another person. At your age and with your knowledge, you should have your own company with people working for you. Then you could get all the women you could ever want. Trust me, young man, that girl is rich, and all rich girls believe their wealth can get them any man at any time. I know you're in love, but I could change your life forever. Perhaps God wants it this way; who knows," Watkins told him.

"How do you plan to use the information that you're asking me for?" Deon asked.

"That's none of your business," Watkins said coldly. "All I want you to do is provide me with the information. I don't care if you're stupid enough to tell her or just walk away from me."

"No, sir, I won't do that. I need to think some things over. I'll call you tomorrow," Deon said.

"Well, you won't find me. I don't want to talk to you anymore. But if you get all the information together I asked you for and it's correct, there will be a cool three hundred thousand dollar check waiting for you. My assistant will look over the information you bring to me, and if it's what I want, he'll give you the check. From then on I don't know you, you never saw me, and this will stay between us. I hope you know and understand that I'm a man of my word," Watkins told him.

Deon left with the words *three hundred thousand dollars* ringing in the back of his mind. He went straight to a little bar a block away from the office and ordered a bottle of Heineken. He sat there sipping his beer and thinking about what he should do. He wondered if what Watkins had said about rich women was true. He wondered what people were saying about him behind his back. But the big question was whether this was a joke or just a big setup because three hundred thousand dollars was a lot of money.

Deon didn't see Mary that day. The following day he got up and called Watkins's assistant.

After much thought, and finding the lure of the money irresistible, he decided to do what Watkins had asked without any regard for the impact it might have on Mary and her children's lives—the same children he had been calling his own. He picked up a computer disk and slipped it in his briefcase before going to work. He went into Mary's office, kissed her, and played around a little to make her laugh before going back to his desk to start work.

At noon, blaming a heavy workload, Deon refused to go out with Mary for lunch, which was something they had been doing for a long time. He stayed behind in the office, took out his computer disk, and copied all of the company information. He returned the disk to its case and hid it in his pocket.

At the end of the day, Deon told Mary he was going home to clean up his apartment, but she wanted to spend the rest of the day with him. He again refused, saying that his apartment was too messy for anyone to see. He promised that he would come to her place in a couple of hours because he would do the work quickly. They both left work, but Deon went to use the pay phone at the corner of the street. He called Watkins's assistant and asked him to meet him, but the assistant refused; Deon should come to their office so the disk could be verified with all the necessary information.

"But what if I come there and you forcibly take the disk away from me? I would be left with nothing," Deon told him.

"That's not how we do business. Remember, you're talking to legitimate businessmen. We aren't the Mafia. We deal in trust, and it was trust that brought my boss this far and has made him a multibillionaire," he told Deon.

"OK, I'm on my way."

The disk was verified, and they made the exchange. The assistant told him to spend the money well, but if he leaked any of the information, he might get himself killed. Deon took his advice very seriously and went straight to his bank to deposit the check before going back to stay with his fiancée that night. Deon was still wondering how Watkins was going to use the information.

Watkins and his associates worked around the clock to find a way to bankrupt Mary's company. With the information Deon provided, they were ready to do all the damage they possibly could.

Watkins knew the manager at the branch of the bank that Mary's company used. He called him to set up a meeting. Watkins told him what he wanted to do to Mary's company, and he promised to pay him well for his help. Mr. Brown Wallace, the bank manager, told him it would be very easy; he could break the company up in no time. He gave him all the secret details about transferring money and closing out accounts.

Chapter 32

Watkins quickly set up an office in Detroit, Michigan, that same week, using the information he had obtained. He installed the equipment he would need to decimate Mary's company. With the help of Brown, they cleared Mary's account of all her money and effectively closed it down. They transferred the money through several different bank accounts until the money ended up in the Bahamas. This way nobody would know where it was, and not even the FBI would be able to trace it. Cleverly, this was all done using Mary's information.

The company was now broke, and with almost three million dollars in outstanding loans, which Watkins had also taken out in the company's name, the bank had no choice but to send a letter to Mary telling her that it wanted her to pay back the amount of the loan that she owed.

When Mary received the letter from the bank, she went wild and called Brown, but unfortunately there was nothing he could do to help. He said he wanted her to return the money the bank had loaned her.

Mary called her lawyer, and he tried to get the bank to give her more time, but he ended up having to take things to court. Mary's company lost the case. They appealed the decision and lost that too. Mary was devastated. She was ordered to pay back every dime her company owed the bank. If this couldn't be done, their property would have to be sold to settle the outstanding loan.

When the company finally did go bankrupt, the story hit the newspaper, and Watkins thanked his men for their help. Nobody suspected that Watkins had anything to do with it. Deon broke off the relationship; he was too guilty to stay around. Deon move back to Quebec City, Quebec, with his money. Mary was left totally alone with no one to talk to except her children and her lawyer. She came to the decision that she had no choice but to put her company up for sale, but no one would pay her the kind of money she was asking for—until Watkins came along and made a generous offer. When she agreed to his offer, Watkins paid the bank the money she owed and paid her an additional five million dollars for the company and the land it occupied.

Mary no longer had her business or her fiancée, but she had five million dollars in the bank. After paying the outstanding wages to all of her employees, she was left with $3.5 million dollars. She still couldn't understand how this had all happened. She hadn't done anything wrong; however, no answers came to her. Unaware of the circumstances, Solomon went to visit his children as well as Mary. She had changed, and he felt sorry for her because she was still the mother of his children. At first Mary refused to tell him anything that was going on in her life, but after a while she poured out the whole story, no longer able to hold back the truth or her emotions.

The story saddened Solomon deeply. "Look, I still have feelings for you, and I am prepared to help you out in any way I can. If possible I would like you and our children to come to Chicago and stay there with me. We'll put the past behind us so we can move on with a new life. I'll take good care of you. All I want is for you to trust me. I don't want our two beautiful children to grow up seeing their parents apart. If we stay together, we can watch them grow up the way we want them to. I love you like I love them."

Tears rolled from her eyes. "I'd like you to give me some time to think about this and come back next week. Perhaps you should take the children and spend a week with them if you like," she told him.

"That's what I've been waiting to hear all along. Let me call the airline and arrange their tickets."

He took out his cell phone, but Mary interrupted him.

"But that was just something I was thinking about. I didn't mean to say that you could take them now," Mary said.

"Please, let me take them. This is the best thing you could ever do for me right now. I want you to have some time to think about the things we talked about," Solomon said.

"OK, you can take them for this week, but you must promise me that you'll bring them back the following weekend," she warned.

"I promise," Solomon replied.

Mary got a sheet of paper and wrote down in big black letters, "I promise to keep my children for only one week, and I will bring them back on Saturday." She asked Solomon to date and sign it.

"Why are you doing this? Why do you want me to go through this again?" Solomon asked her.

She looked at him. "If you think you'll do as you've said, then I see no reason why you wouldn't sign this."

"OK." Solomon took the paper and signed it.

That week was one of the best of Solomon's life. He spoiled his children by giving them everything they wanted. Their rooms weren't big enough to hold it all. Even his grandparents had a great time with their great-grandchildren and were hoping they could stay longer than the week, but Solomon told them the promise he had made.

While Solomon and the children were outside playing basketball, one of his maids ran to him, telling him that he had a phone call. He asked her to take a message.

"It's very important. Someone is calling from New York, and I already told them that you were out here playing with your children," the maid said.

The look on her face told him it was serious, so he went to answer it. The person on the phone introduced himself as a police officer from New York. When Solomon heard this, he thought perhaps it was because of his children, so he quickly told the officer that he was going to be returning the children as he had promised.

"I know the paper that you're talking about. That's why we are calling you. It's not because of your children. It's because of their mother. She is dead. We believe it was a suicide, but we are continuing to investigate the circumstances that led up to her death. We would like you to return to New York as soon as possible with the children because we have some questions for all of you," the officer said.

Solomon was stunned by the news, but he told the officer, "OK, I'll be there first thing tomorrow morning with the children."

"OK, we'll be waiting to pick you up when you arrive at the airport," the officer told him.

Solomon hung up the phone and dropped down into the chair with his hands on his head moaning, "Why? Why? Why?" The children overheard him and came in asking, "What's wrong, Daddy?" He looked at the children. He held them in his arms as the tears ran down his face. The children grew concerned and wanted to know why he was crying. He told them to wait there and that he would be right back. He went to his bedroom and picked up the phone. He called Mr. Carter and told him of Mary's death. Mr. Carter advised Solomon not to tell the children for the time being but perhaps wait until they got back to New York.

"I'll meet you at the airport tomorrow and pick you up myself, so that we can talk about what to do. At least I'll be by your side to make sure you and the children are all right," Mr. Carter told him.

"But, sir, the officer who gave me the message told me that he would be picking me up from the airport," Solomon replied.

"Don't worry about it. I'll come and pick you up. Right now I want you to go back and play with the kids and try not to be too upset in front of them," Mr. Carter said.

"OK, thank you. I'll see you tomorrow," Solomon told him.

Solomon asked his maid to take the children upstairs to his grandparents' place so they could stay there for the night. He would pick them up in the morning.

"I just want to be alone right now," he told her.

Solomon stayed downstairs. He sobbed as he reminisced about how he and Mary had first met and how they had been so in love with each other. Then his thinking shifted to what had caused Mary to take her own life. Did she really have as many problems as she had told him? He had told her that he was willing to help her in any way possible. Could she not have just trusted his word? His thoughts were all over the place, and that night he didn't sleep very well. His grief was too much.

The next morning he went upstairs to wake his children and bring them down to be bathed and dressed. He told them they were going back to New York, and they were very happy that they would be going to see their mother. He didn't want the children to ask too many questions, so he made himself busy by preparing their breakfast and packing their bags. When the time came, they drove to the airport for their flight to New York.

When they got to New York, both the police officer and Mr. Carter were there to pick them up. Solomon refused to ride with the police officer and instead went with Mr. Carter; the officer followed behind. They arrived at Mary's house, leaving the children to wait in the car. The officer also came in and asked Solomon to come with him so they could talk. Solomon turned to Mr. Carter. He asked him to go back to the car and wait with the children.

"Tell them their dad is a little busy. When I finish with the police, you and I have to talk about some important things."

Chapter 33

Mr. Carter went out to the car to see the children, and Solomon's son asked about his mother and said he wanted to see her. Mr. Carter told them she wasn't there, and he didn't know where she had gone, but they would wait in the car together.

Solomon sat with the police officer, Sgt. Keneral, who took out his notebook and said, "I'm sorry about the death of your children's mother. I just need to ask you a few questions. You're not a suspect here, and we are not charging you with any crime. We are just getting as much information as we possibly can. How long have you known Mary?" Keneral asked.

"About fourteen years now," Solomon replied.

"How would you describe your relationship during the time of your marriage?"

"We had a wonderful relationship. She was a lovely lady, and I loved her very much. When our children were born, it made me love her even more," he answered.

"Has she ever tried to commit suicide or harm herself or anybody else?"

"Not at all," Solomon replied.

"Do you know or have you any idea why she would have killed herself? Anything at all?"

Solomon told Keneral everything Mary had said on the day he went to visit the children.

"Do you have anything else you want to add?"

"All I want to say is that she was a wonderful woman. I'll miss her always," Solomon replied.

"Have you told your children?" Officer Keneral asked Solomon.

"Not yet. I'm afraid to tell them because I don't know what their reaction will be," Solomon replied.

"Well, I'd tell them now because they need to know what's going on. We're trying to locate other members of her family, but the only one we've found at this time didn't want to have anything to with the situation. Are you prepared to keep the children with you and care for them?" Sgt. Keneral asked.

"Of course! They're my children, and I love them more than anything in the world," Solomon replied.

Once they were finished, Solomon and the officer went to call the children inside to break the news to them about their mother's death.

The children then realized they would never see their mother again. They were plunged into devastation and disbelief, so arrangements were made to take them to the mortuary to see their mother's body. It was a very sad time.

That day Solomon shaved his head, and so did his son.

They went back to the house. Solomon packed all of the children's stuff into a rental truck and had everything transported to his house in Chicago. Solomon and Mr. Carter flew back to Chicago with the children. Mr. Carter stayed a week with them before returning to New York. Solomon and his children were living together as a family now.

A week later, Sgt. Keneral called. When Solomon picked up the phone, the officer apologized for taking so long to call him back.

"With regard to the question you asked me, we've checked it out and found that your ex-wife didn't have any life insurance policy with an insurance company registered in the United States. I'm sorry about that, but at least you have your children back now." The officer said good-bye and hung up.

Solomon was still seeing Julianne Gorier off and on after his divorce. She had come to Chicago several times to help look after Solomon's children. Solomon needed to find another mother for his lovely kids, but the only person who came to his mind was Julianne. He called her and asked if she would consider moving in with him and his children in Chicago.

"I told you a long time ago that I wanted us to live together, but you refused. You know that I love you, and I would love to take care of your children because I love them too. Nothing would make me happier than coming to live in the house with you," Julianne replied.

Solomon was overjoyed and couldn't wait to tell his children the news. They, too, were happy.

***

Three years had passed since Solomon's ex-wife passed away. One day he was sitting in the backyard with his fiancée, Julianne, watching the children play in the swimming pool. His maid came and told him that there was a man named Deon from Quebec City waiting to speak with him. Solomon excused himself. He went to the front door, and when he saw Deon, he was pleased and hugged him happily.

They sat in Solomon's living room. "So what brings you here today, and how did you find me in the first place?" Solomon asked.

"Your ex-wife had given me your address and phone number some time ago, and then I found out that she was dead," Deon replied. "I was so sorry to hear that because I told her I was willing to help her pay off her debts and restart her business. I knew she was having difficulties, but I guess there were other personal issues involved.

"I wanted to say thank-you for the kindness you showed me when I was working for you and your wife. I also wanted to apologize for the way I set you up against your wife with Julianne, which caused your divorce. Your wife was beautiful, and I wanted her. To be honest, we were in love with each other while you two were still married. This started long before you had your children," Deon confessed.

Confused, Solomon asked, "Are you serious?"

"Yes, I am serious. I'm telling you the truth. In fact, those children aren't even yours. They are my biological children. We arranged for a DNA test four years ago." With that he pulled out a copy of the DNA test and handed it to Solomon.

Solomon took it and read it over before tearing it up in a fit of rage.

"Is this why you came to see me? I took care of you. I supported you and gave you everything you ever asked me for. I treated you like my own brother. I don't believe a word you're saying. You had better take me to court. I believe they are mine, and I think you're just lying to me. Now please leave my house and don't ever come back around me; otherwise, I'll be forced to shoot you." He grabbed the coffee cup out of Deon's hand.

"I think we are going to have to go to court to settle this, and you might regret your decision," Deon told him and walked out the door.

Solomon slammed the door behind him and told his maid never to let that man into the house again. Although the visit from Deon had spoiled the whole weekend, he concealed his feelings from everyone.

As his daughter's eleventh birthday was approaching, they decided to throw a party and invite all of her classmates. Everyone had a great time, but the next morning Solomon received a summons from the court, commanding him to appear on a specific date. Solomon set up an appointment with his lawyer, Mr. Steven Arora. His lawyer advised him to take the DNA test so he would have evidence to prove to the court that the children were his biological children. Solomon refused because he was afraid things might turn out for the worst. His lawyer agreed, and they decided they would go to court, hear what was said at the preliminary hearing, and take it from there.

Mr. Carter was at the courthouse by Solomon's side, along with his grandparents. The two men presented their case before a judge, but at the end of the hearing, the judge ordered that the two men undertake a DNA test. On the day of their DNA testing, Solomon and Deon showed up with their lawyers.

Chapter 34

Solomon's lawyer called him into one of the anterooms. He told him to stay calm and not to worry about anything. "I'm sure the results will be positive for us, and then you'll be able to file charges against this man for trying to steal your children away from you," Steven told him.

They went out of the room and sat with the children. The judge told them that nothing more needed to be discussed; all the answers to his questions were on the paper he was holding in his hand. "I won't waste any more of your time or mine, so I'll get directly to the point. From the results it is 99.99 percent conclusive that the biological father of the two children in question here is Deon."

The pronouncement hit Solomon like a ton of bricks, and he passed out, falling to the floor. When he came to himself, the judge asked him with concern, "Are you all right, sir?"

"Yes, I'm fine," replied Solomon.

The judge took his seat once again.

"On the basis of these DNA results, the court orders that the two children be turned over to their biological father at once. However, since you have acted in the capacity of their father since their birth, I'm ordering that the children be able to spend one last week with you before you are required to return them to their biological father. That is the verdict of this court," the judge announced with a final, solemn bang of the gavel.

Solomon was shaking like a leaf and crying desperately. His fiancée and his grandparents were all very upset. Nobody could believe the verdict. Solomon ran out of the court and hailed a taxi to take him home. Julianne and Solomon's grandparents gathered up the children and brought them back to the house, knowing they would only have another week together.

Solomon was devastated. This was the worst day of his life, and he didn't want to talk to anyone. Julianne called Mr. Carter. She broke the news to him, and he too was crestfallen and shaken. Julianne and the children fell asleep on the couch, waiting for Solomon to come out and talk to them.

For the entire week, Solomon was trapped in a miserable state of mind. He even went out and bought a gun. He asked the children if they would like to go fishing. He had the maid prepare a lunch and gather up all their fishing equipment. Solomon hid the gun in his car. They drove to the lake, and Solomon handed the children their fishing equipment. He warned them that if they caught a fish, they shouldn't kill it but put it in the bucket of water and keep it alive. Once they were in position, he sat down to have a cigarette, and the children were very surprised because they had never seen Solomon smoke before.

Solomon just sat there. He was planning to kill the children and himself. He thought back to when they were first born and how he had watched them grow; he thought about all the difficult times he'd had and the risks he had undergone just to see them. He thought about the love he had for them and the way they used to play together. He picked up the gun, but when he saw the little boy, Bobby, and his sister having such a good time, he put it back down beside him. At that moment a chill ran through his body, and he took the gun back to his car and hid it. He decided to fish with the children. He only had a little bit more time left.

The following day Solomon prepared all the checks for the money he had been saving for his children to give to Deon in the presence of the judge. He told the nurse and the maid that he wouldn't require their services anymore. He paid them the wages that he owed them. They weren't happy, but nothing more could be done. The bags were packed with all of the children's belongings, and there was a great deal of sadness in the house. They cried every time they looked at their father.

That night Solomon prayed. "Lord God, I don't need a fortune. I don't need riches. Send down your angels, Lord, to help me during this difficult time in my life. I don't want my children to leave me." He went to bed hoping that God was listening up above.

The next morning Solomon and Julianne loaded the children in the SUV with all of their belongings. His grandparents were ready with the children. Solomon gathered up all the documents he had prepared for the children's future. They all got in the van, and he drove to the courthouse. As ordered by the judge, he turned the children over to their biological father with all of the documents and checks for his children's future that he had set aside for them, but Deon refused to accept the money. He threw it back at him. They left the court.

Deon and his wife drove to the airport with the children. A court officer accompanied them to make sure that the children did not run away. They all flew to Quebec City.

Solomon's family brought him home.

***

"I'm pregnant!" Julianne finally told Solomon eight months after he lost his children to Deon. Solomon didn't believe her and grew suddenly angry.

"How can I be sure the baby is mine?"

They ended up having a big argument. She left him and arranged to have a DNA test done when the baby was born to prove that Solomon was the father. Julianne was too far along in her pregnancy to even consider having an abortion, and it was too difficult for Solomon to think about trusting anybody again.

A week or so after Julianne left Solomon, she returned to the house to see him.

"What are you doing here?" Solomon asked.

"I can't believe you! After all the years we've been together, I clean your house, I cook for you, we have sex anytime you want, and I do whatever you ask me to do. I have dedicated my life to you, and this is how you treat me!" she cried.

"Look, woman, I don't know why you came here today and what makes you think you can just come into my house and tell me what you feel," Solomon told her.

"This is my house too. I live here. We both furnished and decorated it together. I don't want your money; all I want is you. I love you. I want to be your wife and bear your children. If you want, we can do a DNA test when I give birth. I want you to know that I'm not the same as your deceitful wife. Even if you don't trust me, think about the happiness we had together and all the things I did for you," she replied.

"Look, any woman would do the same thing. You people can cut the heart out of a man's chest, and he won't realize it until it's too late. All I want right now is for you to stay away from me until your baby is born. After the DNA results are in, we will then know the type of person you are. Can you do that for me?" Solomon begged her.

She just looked at him and cried as she left to go back to her mother's house in New York.

Two weeks later Mr. Carter came to visit Solomon.

"Oh! Here you are. I wasn't expecting you; you didn't call to tell me you were coming," Solomon told him.

"That's something I don't think is necessary. I want you to know that there's something eating me up, which I need to tell you about, and although I'm a little afraid of what you'll do to me afterward, I'll have to take my chances," Mr. Carter told him.

Chapter 35

"What are you talking about?" Solomon asked. "I've never heard you talk like this before. Come in and have a seat. Can I get you something to eat or drink? I can make your favorite sandwich. You know I'm good at it," Solomon said.

"As a matter of fact, I would like a nice cup of coffee with milk and that sandwich you were talking about," Mr. Carter replied.

Solomon quickly prepared the sandwich and brought it to him.

"You're right. It's just the way I like it." He savored every bite.

"You know what? I want you to take me to the best bar around here 'cause I'd love a cold beer," Mr. Carter said.

"Just give me a few minutes to get changed."

Solomon quickly went upstairs and changed. He told his grandparents that he was going to town with Mr. Carter, and they could call him on his cell phone if they needed anything. He went back downstairs and told Mr. Carter that he was ready.

"Where's your fiancée, Juliane? I haven't seen her since I got here," Mr. Carter asked.

"Well, she's not around here anymore. I don't need a woman around me. I'm quite happy living alone," Solomon replied.

They drove Solomon's Lincoln Navigator to a bar downtown that he frequented after a hard day of work. The waitresses all knew him. He parked just down the street, and they walked back. The look on Mr. Carter's face told him that something wasn't quite right.

"You all right, Carter?" Solomon asked.

"Oh yes, I'm fine. Why do you ask?" Mr. Carter said.

"It looks like something is bothering you. Something is bothering me too. I can't really think straight at the moment. Maybe it's good for the two of us to be in this mood. Let's just go in here and have some fun. You can tell me whatever it is you want to tell me afterward," Solomon told him.

"That's right," Mr. Carter agreed.

The bar was packed with jovial people sitting and drinking, playing pool, and happily enjoying themselves.

"Wow! This place looks different. I'm feeling a little different now," Mr. Carter said.

"What do you mean?"

"I just started feeling a little differently. Let's go and have some drinks and forget our worries. This is going to be my treat," Mr. Carter said.

"No you don't. You're in Chicago, and that's a long way from New York. This is my territory, so I'll be the one who's paying for everything. New York money doesn't work here in Chicago," Solomon told him.

"This is the United States, and we're using the same currency." Mr. Carter said.

Solomon just stared at him and said, "I'm only joking."

They walked to the counter, and Mr. Carter ordered a Bud Light beer. Solomon ordered three shots of Gordon's gin with orange juice.

They moved to the poolroom after Mr. Carter mentioned he didn't know how to play. There, the subject turned to girls, and though Mr. Carter said he was a married man who wasn't interested in doing anything, he might like to take a look.

After the game Solomon spoke to the girl at the desk and asked her to have the girls come out so Mr. Carter could see them.

Mr. Carter turned to Solomon and said, "Look, I only want to have a look at what you're talking about. I have no intentions of having any sex with a prostitute."

"Come on, you're always busy working up there in New York; you never have time to really enjoy yourself. Well, just have a look. I'm not going to force you to have fun," Solomon said with a smile.

The receptionist came in and told them to follow her. She went into a room and all the girls were standing there.

"Oh my! Can I touch them?" Mr. Carter asked with a smile on his face.

"Sure, go ahead, touch their breasts and butts if you want to. Then you can choose whatever lady you want, and you can be sure she'll treat you right," the woman said.

Mr. Carter happily started checking out all the girls. When he was finished, he went back to Solomon.

"Oh boy! Those girls are beautiful. I think I might change my mind. I'm here to have some fun. I'm going to go all the way, but now I'm confused because they're all so beautiful. I've never touched so many beautiful women in my life before."

"I know that feeling," the receptionist said.

"You should close your eyes and make a decision. Pick one, two, or as many of them as you want. I'm warning you—we're not sleeping here. We have about three hours to enjoy the ladies," Solomon told him.

Mr. Carter looked around; he finally chose three of the women and was then escorted to a beautiful bedroom. Solomon bought two bottles of champagne and took them to the bedroom. He told Mr. Carter to enjoy himself.

"Aren't you taking any of the girls?" he asked Solomon.

"I already picked my favorite girl, and she's waiting for me right now."

They both laughed. Solomon closed the door and went to his room. The three hours quickly turned into five.

When they eventually returned home, Solomon's grandparents came downstairs to visit with Mr. Carter and him. Solomon asked his grandmother if she could prepare him some soup. When it was ready, he and Mr. Carter each had a bowl. It made them feel much better. After drinking some champagne, they all sat and talked. Mr. Carter then turned to Solomon and told him that he still had something very important to say.

"Oh yes, I forgot about that. Do you want to go into the backyard or would you prefer we sit here?"

"Anywhere you like; it doesn't matter."

Solomon asked his grandparents to excuse him. They told him they were going for a walk.

"Wait." Solomon reached into his pocket and handed them some money. They thanked him and went for their walk. Solomon made sure they were gone so they couldn't eavesdrop on his conversation with Mr. Carter.

"OK, you can tell me whatever it is you want to tell me, and if you need my help, you know I'm prepared to do anything I possibly can," Solomon told him.

He sat down and waited for Mr. Carter to speak. He was thinking that it was probably about an investment or business venture because it seemed to be important to Mr. Carter.

"Please promise me that you'll not get angry with me until I'm finished telling you what I have to say," Mr. Carter said.

"I promise," replied Solomon.

"This is about your mother," Carter told him.

"OK," he replied.

Mr. Carter looked rather sad as he continued. "When you were arrested and in the hands of Sten, I was arrested as well; they found out about my connection to your family. Sten threatened to destroy my family and my businesses if I didn't cooperate with them. I told them everything that I knew about you, but I didn't tell them that I knew where you hid the documents. They were talking about destroying all your relatives, one by one, until they found what they were searching for.

"They thought they would be able to locate your mother and grandparents. When things started getting out of hand, I came to see your grandparents, and we discussed everything. It was then that we finally decided to kill your mother so that everybody would be safe. We thought that with her out of the way, the whole case would be closed. I couldn't afford to lose the business that my family and I had worked so hard to build up. It was our whole life. I wasn't prepared to destroy it for something I wouldn't benefit from."

Solomon was incredulous and felt rage building up in him, but he strained to remain calm. "Excuse me," he said and went into the kitchen for a glass of water. He came back, sat down, and told Mr. Carter to continue.

"You know that I had been in love with your mother from the very first day I met her. I went to your mother's house. At that time I had a spare key for the house that she had given to me a long time ago. I opened the door slowly, and I hid in the hall with a baseball bat; it was dark because the lights were off. When she came out, I hit her in the back of the head. She fell to the floor unconscious."

Chapter 36

Solomon stood up and looked at Mr. Carter. He wasn't sure if he was being serious or joking. He thought to himself that maybe Mr. Carter was just trying to goad him into getting angry, but when he looked at his eyes, he couldn't tell. He sat back down; he was breathing very hard in an attempt to keep his temper.

Mr. Carter continued. "While she was lying there, I kept hitting her on the head with the baseball bat until I was sure she was dead. Then I went and brought the bomb got from Sten, I and placed it beside her. I left and drove a couple of yards down the street, and then I triggered the bomb.

"I parked near a soccer field and waited for the bomb to go off, and when it did, the whole house was blown to bits. Sten knew all about it. Everything I was doing for the FBI to solve the case was all a show. The murder was well planned, and nobody will ever find any evidence. I did all of this to protect you because the government still believes that you should be killed. They're still planning the perfect way to kill you."

Solomon could bear no more. He snapped, and in his fury, he punched him hard in the face, shattering his nose. He quickly ran to a cupboard near the television and pulled out his pistol, pointing it at Mr. Carter's head.

When Mr. Carter saw the gun, he said, "You're right to want to kill me, but I don't think this is the right time because the police will put you in jail for life—if they don't send you to death row. Think about your children. I know you love them, and you want to see them. Think about your business."

"Shut up!" Solomon said, and he struck him with the butt of the pistol in the head.

Carter fell backward and cried out, "I'm sorry, I thought I was helping you!"

"You knew I loved my mother. She was the only person in the world apart from my children that I loved. You took her away from me. She never did you any harm. She was an innocent woman." Solomon was crying and hitting Mr. Carter, who begged for forgiveness.

All Solomon could think about was his mother; he had lost his children, and now his grandparents had betrayed him by helping murder his lovely mother. He cried bitterly, and Mr. Carter tried to comfort him, but Solomon pushed him away.

"Go away! I don't ever want to see you again in my life. If I ever lay my eyes on you again, I'll kill you. Just get out of my house! Go… Go…"

He started kicking and hitting him and finally pushed him out the door so hard that he fell down on the grass. Mr. Carter picked himself up and ran for his life.

Mr. Carter had actually killed Mrs. Brownell, thinking it was Clare, Solomon's mother. He didn't know that Clare had secretly traveled to Sweden a few weeks back without telling anybody, including Mr. Carter.

Solomon was still sitting in the living room crying when his grandparents returned from their walk. They saw all the blood on the floor. When his grandparents saw him, they cried out, "Oh my God! What happened to you?"

Solomon stood up, still holding the gun in his hand. "Sit down. I want to ask you a serious question, and I want a serious answer right now."

His grandparents looked in his eyes and saw that he wasn't joking; they were afraid. They sat down beside each other, shaking and praying that he wouldn't do anything stupid with the gun.

"Did you plan with Mr. Carter to kill my mother?" he asked.

"Calm down, son," his grandfather said.

"Don't tell me to calm down! I want you to answer me right now."

Frightened to death, they confessed to everything that had happened. It was exactly as Mr. Carter had told him.

"I thought you were my grandparents!" Solomon exclaimed. "You claimed to love my mother. When none of your other children would see you, my mother was there for you, giving you everything you needed. She looked after your daily needs. Now I know that everything you told me about my mother was all a lie. You live in my house and eat my food. I take care of you. I want you to go back to your room, pack all of your belongings as quickly as possible, and get out of my house. I don't want to see your faces ever again."

"But, son, you don't want to do that. We have nowhere else to go," his grandmother said.

"I don't care where you go. Just do what I say."

They quickly went upstairs to pack their clothes while Solomon waited downstairs. Without Solomon knowing, his grandparents called the police and told them that their grandson had attacked them. The police told them they were on their way.

Something told Solomon to put the gun away, so he took it out to the backyard and hid it among the flowers. When he came back inside, he cleaned the blood from the floors.

"Are you guys finished?" he called up to his grandparents. "Hurry up!"

A knock came to the door, and thinking it was Mr. Carter, Solomon said, "Go away. I don't want to talk to you."

Then a deep voice shot back, "Open the door. It's the police. If you don't open the door, we will break it down."

Solomon quickly abided. Two police officers entered the home.

"We received a call from someone telling us that they were being attacked."

His grandparents came downstairs, and his grandfather spoke. "This is the young man who is trying to kill us. He had a gun."

"I don't have a gun. I don't know what they're talking about. All I told them was that I didn't want them in my house any longer. I want them to leave right away."

"Are these your relatives?" one of the officers asked.

"Yes, they're my grandparents, but I have disowned them. I want them to leave my house."

"I don't think we understand what has happened. You're throwing them out at a time like this? What have they done?"

"Well, sir, I don't have any explanation to give you right now, but I want you to understand that this house is my property. I don't want them here. Is that simple and clear?"

"Where's the gun?" the other officer asked.

"What gun are you talking about, sir?"

"The gun you threatened them with. If you don't give it to us, we'll have to search your house and find it ourselves," the officer replied.

"What gun? I don't have a gun. You're welcome to check the whole house if you want."

"Your grandparents told us that you did. We believe them," the officer said.

"Why would you believe them? Can't you see how old they are? They don't know what they're talking about. Please, officer, don't listen to them."

"We know what we saw, and we're not crazy. Being old doesn't make you crazy," his grandmother replied.

The officer asked Solomon to take a seat in the chair and relax while they searched his house. They searched through the living room and his bedroom as well as the kitchen and bathroom, but they didn't find the gun.

"OK, we've checked everywhere in the house. We haven't seen any weapons. Now are you absolutely sure you saw him with a gun?" the officer asked his grandparents.

"Yes, sir. He was holding a gun and pointing it at us. We're not lying."

"Well, we didn't find a gun," the officer said.

"I told you they weren't telling you the truth," Solomon said.

"Why don't you people tell me what this is all about so we can try and settle the problem?" the officer said.

While the officers had been searching the house for the gun, his grandparents had already decided that they wouldn't tell the police anything; otherwise, they might be charged with murder.

When they pressed Solomon on what occurred, he told them, "Nothing happened, but I'm sick and tired of looking at them."

"What do you mean? Are they abusive? Do they leave your house dirty? Do they complain all the time, or have they destroyed anything that was important to you?" they asked Solomon.

"Yes, they destroyed something very important to me," Solomon replied.

"What was that?" the officer asked.

"It's personal," he replied. Then he went silent.

The police went back to speak to his grandparents.

"Did you destroy something important to your grandson?"

"Not that we know of," they lied.

There wasn't anything more to say. The police left, and the grandparents cleared out. The house was empty and silent again. Solomon got up and went to lock the door. When he looked around at the mess the officers had left in his house, he stood with his hands on his head and yelled loudly. It took him a week to put everything back in place, but at least he was still putting in a lot of time managing his supermarket.

Chapter 37

The next weeks involved severing old ties and burning bridges. Solomon arranged to change the name of his businesses. He purchased a condo in downtown Chicago and sold his house. He really regretted selling the house because it was built on the site where his mother had died. He had wanted to keep her memory alive, but he realized that it was probably the best thing he could do in order to save his sanity. He changed his looks by putting on some extra weight and growing a beard.

Though he missed his grandparents, the damage was already done; their relationship was irreparable. He stopped going to all the places he used to go; he found some new places to frequent when he wanted to go out after work. He cut himself off from his friends, and now his only friend was his job.

While working one afternoon on his scheduling, he heard a knock at his door. This was unusual because his receptionist usually buzzed him to tell him who was there. He got up and answered the knock. His ex-fiancée stood there with a small baby in her arms.

"Oh my God! How did you get past the receptionist?"

"She knows me," Julianne said as she walked past him to take a seat.

"Look, I am kind of busy right now, so why don't I talk to you tonight after work?" Solomon suggested.

"I am not leaving here until we get things settled about your son," she told him.

"Is this your baby?" Solomon asked her, looking at the child with adoring eyes. "He is beautiful. I am sorry for any grief I caused you, but I was very downhearted at that time."

"OK, I'll be waiting for your call tonight." She kissed him and went back home.

But Solomon had no intention of calling her or trying to see her. He didn't even think about her. Julianne waited for a couple of weeks; she finally couldn't wait any longer. She decided it was time to take Solomon to court so he would start looking after his son financially.

When Solomon was served with the summons, he decided not to hire a lawyer; he planned to defend himself. He told the judge that he didn't trust his fiancée; therefore he couldn't believe 100 percent that the baby was in fact his son, and the judge ordered them to submit to paternity tests.

Two weeks later the tests were revealed in court. It was 99.99 percent conclusive that Solomon was the father of Jason, Julianne's child.

"I have a son. I finally have a son." Without thinking, Solomon ran over to the judge. He hugged and kissed him. Everyone in the courtroom was taken aback by his behavior.

"I'll do whatever you want me to do for my boy." He turned to Julianne. "You know that I love you, and what happened in the past made me afraid that it might happen again. I was so scared. Please forgive me. I do love you."

Solomon and Julianne settled their differences and started living together again in his new condo. Solomon did not intend to marry her yet; he still felt he couldn't trust her completely. He told Julianne, "I don't want you to give up. I love you, and I'll not give up either. We will try to have more children and be a happy family."

A year later the two of them were finally married, and things were going well. Julianne was trying very hard to ignore her husband's mistrust. He didn't want her to have friends, and he was secretive.

She didn't realize just how much he didn't trust her until she had to undergo DNA testing three different times at three different locations every time they got into a fight. She actually thought he might be a little crazy because of his need to make sure of his bloodline.

She felt she wasn't free and that Solomon was controlling her. She was getting a little sick and tired of it, and their once happy union devolved into discontentment. She filed for divorce. The court ordered that Julianne have full custody of Jason, and Solomon was allowed weekend visits.

He loved his son so much, but when Jason was seven, Solomon started teaching him not to ever trust anybody—not even his mother. He told him what had happened to him in his first marriage and how he had lost his children when they were taken to Canada. Jason was sorry to hear about the suffering that his father had gone through, and he started believing what he was saying to him. Whenever he returned home from visiting his father, Jason asked Julianne all kinds of strange questions, and this made her wonder what Solomon was telling him. Jason had been asking questions that children wouldn't normally ask.

***

Solomon had finally settled down and was happy with his life. He had his own child now, and he didn't plan to ever get married again or get involved in another serious relationship with any other woman. He had decided just to take care of Jason and watch him grow. He worked hard at his business. *One day he might even see his other children again,* he thought.

After one very long, trying day, Solomon decided to go to his usual hangout for a drink. He still had a few friends whom he usually met there. He thought he might have a nice massage and some fun with the beautiful ladies.

He ordered two shots of vodka with ice. While they were being poured, he looked around and saw a good friend, Abraham Woloski, who looked sad; he was nursing his drink. Solomon said to the bartender, "I'll be at that table with my friend, so you can bring my drinks over there when they're ready." He walked over to his friend.

Usually they greeted each other with excitement and maybe a few jokes, but that didn't happen. Solomon knew something had happened to Abraham.

"Are you OK?" he asked.

"Do I look OK to you?" Abraham replied.

"What happened? I've never seen you looking like this," Solomon said.

"My girlfriend left me for another man," Abraham replied. His eyes were red like he had been crying.

It seemed bad luck was striking everybody these days. Solomon tried to comfort him, telling him to be strong and move on with his life, just as Abraham's girlfriend had done already.

***

Time passed, and Solomon's business was burgeoning. He had become a rich man who could buy whatever he wanted. He started paying more attention to his son—trying to make him happy. He no longer thought about Mr. Carter or his grandparents; he just kept to himself. He never did learn to trust anybody with any of his important secrets.

At work he felt the need to do everything in his own way, and some of his managers even started calling him Mr. Know-It-All. But he didn't care; everything was going in the direction that he wanted it to. He was hardworking and friendly to all of his employees, and he was eager to help anyone who asked him.

He took his favorite photo of his mother and father to an artist and arranged for him to paint a beautiful portrait of them, which he hung in his living room so he could look at them every day to feel their presence around him.

Chapter 38

Many years had passed, and Solomon was living quietly and well. One day his secretary informed him that a man and woman were waiting to see him.

"They say they're from Montreal and that you're their father,' the receptionist told him.

He got out from behind his desk and went to the waiting room. Once he got closer, the two people ran and hugged him happily. Only then did he recognize them. Suddenly Solomon cried. He touched their faces with immense, all-consuming joy.

"I knew you would come back to me one day. I don't know why, but I always felt you were going to show up again. Follow me into my office and let's talk."

He grabbed their hands and brought them back into the office.

"Where are your father and stepmother?"

Bobby, who was now thirty years old, spoke first. "First of all, we want to tell you that he wasn't our father, and we never considered him our dad. As far as we are concerned, we've always looked up to you, and we believe that you're our father. When we were younger, we didn't have the right to do what we wanted because nobody would listen to us. Having to leave with a stranger was probably one of the hardest days of our lives. We didn't get along, and it was a big problem, but my sister, Barbara, who just turned twenty-seven, told me we should remember everything you told us on the day we left for Canada."

"But how did you guys find me?" Solomon asked.

"It wasn't easy. We did everything we could to find you, but everywhere we went they told us your address didn't exist anymore, and we couldn't remember Mr. Carter's address. Our adoptive mother, Sofia, helped us. She took all the information we had and went to an agency. We didn't have a photo of you, which made it all the more difficult. She came to us one afternoon yelling, 'I got it! I found him,' and she gave us the address and phone number of your business. We called the number and confirmed the address before flying out here to Chicago to see you," his daughter Barbara exclaimed.

"Thank God you guys found me. Now tell me everything that has happened to you two." Solomon was pleased.

"When we arrived in Quebec City, we had to learn French. We tried to get used to the Canadian way of life. One day we came home from school, and there were police, fire trucks, and a big crowd of people in front of our house. The police took us to a home for orphaned children without telling us what was going on. We stayed there for several hours until the police came back and told us that our father's wife had caught him in the house having sex with another woman, and she had been so angry that she took out a gun and killed him. She was taken to jail, and that was the last time we saw her. We lived in the orphanage until a woman adopted us. She took care of us like her own children. When she got a job in Montreal, she took us along, and we lived with her until we went to university and graduated," Bobby told him.

"I can't imagine the suffering you've gone through. I don't want you to get angry, but Deon did me wrong; I was an angry man for a long time after that. I am so happy that you're back," Solomon told them. "Where's your adoptive mother now?"

"We left her back at the hotel. She was too tired to come with us and told us that we should come and find you, and then let her know," Barbara said.

"Quick, give me the address of the hotel!"

Solomon asked his secretary to arrange for his driver to go to the hotel and bring her back to the office so he could thank her personally. The driver left immediately.

"How are Grandma and Grandpa?" Bobby asked.

"That's a long story, but I'll tell you. They are very evil people."

Solomon explained everything about how his grandparents and Mr. Carter planned his mother's death. The children were shaken and didn't want to hear anymore.

While they were talking, Solomon's secretary told him that Sofia had arrived. He sent Bobby out to get her. When the two came back to his office, he happily welcomed her and told her to take a seat. Sofia Omnia was a fifty-nine-year-old Bulgarian Canadian. She was a chubby, five-foot-eight woman with black hair and clean white teeth.

"Thank you so very much for adopting my children and taking care of them for all those years," Solomon told her.

"These children were so beautiful, and after hearing about how they were orphaned, I took pity on them. I had no children or husband, so I decided to adopt them as my own," Sofia replied. "Even though I never seemed to have enough money, I got myself a second job and provided them with everything they needed. I wanted them to look presentable in front of their friends. They became Canadian citizens, and they both worked very hard and got good marks in school. I am very proud of them. They always talked about you, so I helped them find you. It took a long five years, but here you are. I'm very pleased that I could help them realize their dreams."

Later they dined out and returned to Solomon's home. He showed them all the things he had bought for them when their birth mother died, and the sight moved them to tears.

Solomon only had three bedrooms in his house, so he gave one each to his son and daughter and told Sofia that she should stay in his room; he would sleep in the living room. It had been a long day for all of them, so they all went to bed.

Sofia returned to Canada after two days, but the kids stayed. Solomon arranged for them to have driving lessons so they could get their licenses. When they passed, he bought each of them a new Toyota Camry and had them insured.

He ordered brochures on various universities across the States so they could choose the school they wanted to attend. He wanted them to go further than getting their master's degree and hoped they would carry on to get a PhD. They were so excited to be back with Solomon that they were prepared to do whatever he told them. They helped him take care of his businesses, and he introduced them to their other brother, Jason, and his mother. They were both very happy to meet them too.

They went to school as planned and completed their PhD's, eventually taking over Solomon's businesses. They helped teach their little brother everything they knew about life and watched him grow up. Solomon had a lot of free time to himself to relax and enjoy the rest of his life. Barbara and Bobby found significant others and married, having children of their own. Sofia died from lung cancer a few years later.

The supermarket business was thriving after having expanded to every major city across the United States, Canada, and Mexico. They were getting richer and richer. When Solomon was about fifty-two years old, he called all his children together. They sat at attention, staring at the old man.

"How happy I am to look and see how God has blessed me with such great children. You're all grown up and have partners of your own. You have all worked hard and have made this company of mine become one of the biggest in the country. Even though I was hard on you, and we've argued many times, we still understand what our focus is. I hope you never lose confidence in the work that you do for this company.

"As you can probably see, I am getting old. But you're all still young and have futures in this company. You've bought your homes and earn your daily bread from this company. I know your children will benefit from it too. I also know that my mother is proud of me because I've used the money left to me wisely and have fulfilled my dream. The money she left me was a great start, and I worked hard toward achieving my goals.

"Hard work pays greatly. If you want something, you have to work for it and believe that you'll get it. If you start thinking negatively about things, you'll give up; and then you won't be able to do what you want, and you'll end up regretting that forever. With the hard work that you have invested, and as long as you look after each other, the business will become one of the world's leading companies, and your future generations will never suffer.

"Love each other, respect each other, and always be there for each other. I won't talk too much on that because I know you love each other, and you would never deliberately hurt one another. You should also help people who are in need and be able to share what you have. I'm not saying that you should just give away the company's money, but do as I always have and set aside money every month for charity.

"I want you to remember that things don't always work out the way you want, but if they don't, don't be frustrated because that's the way life is. You should always have three or more reasons for why you want to do something, and always do the right thing. When you grow bigger, bad things might come your way, and you know how the media can exaggerate things. I'm not worried about that; you've all been prepared for that, and God knows you'll all know what to do.

"Even though I'm not as educated as you are, I'm street smart, and I know my way around the business world. Nobody can fool me because I've done everything you can think of. But this is an old man's story, and I don't think it's important for you to hear, except for what I'm telling you now, but you're all well-educated."

Chapter 39

"It's a small world, and that's why you should never treat another human being like a fool," Solomon continued, imparting his lifetime of wisdom. 'Have respect for everybody, no matter their circumstances. The person you're kind to may be the one who saves your life someday when you need help the most. You think all your friends are happy about the riches that you have, but some of them are praying for evil things to happen to you right now.

"Do you know who your real friends are?" he asked them.

"You," they replied in unison.

"Your real friends are your brothers and sister because they are your blood; they'll always pray for your success, and they will always be there for you. Many years ago my mother wanted to take care of everybody. She wanted to help all her relatives, but it turned back on her. Please don't be like her.

"I didn't borrow any money from any financial institution. I started this business with the money that my mother left for me," Solomon told them.

"You're rich now, and sometimes people will want to be your partner—not for who you are, but for what they can get from you." He looked at his watch. It was time to go back to work. He said that they should speak later at his house. Solomon was strong, and he still helped make decisions for his business.

Solomon went home and took a shower. After eating something he sat in the living room to wait for his children to arrive. An hour or so later, they knocked on his door, and he told them to come inside.

"Well, we're all here, Dad," Barbara said to him.

"This won't take long, I promise," he told them.

"We don't mind. We're happy to listen to you because we have lots of things to learn from you," Barbara said.

"OK."

He walked up to his bedroom and came back with a large envelope. He opened it and took out the documents it contained and put them on the table along with a pen.

His children were wondering what he was doing, but they kept quiet and listened to what he had to say.

"I'll give you the reason why I asked you all to come here. I treat the two of you, Bobby and Barbara, like my very own children. I don't care what other people think; you're my children. I have been watching very closely to see if you would treat your brother, Jason, any differently, but you haven't. I know that the three of you are of one blood and that you love each other. Now I'll be retiring from work so that I can enjoy the fruits of my labor. I have made up my mind as to who should control the business."

He took the document and handed it to Bobby. "You know that in every company there is only one boss, and that is Bobby. From now on he will take over my position. This doesn't mean that the two of you are not a part of this company. You're still owners because when I die, I won't be taking the business with me. It'll belong to all of you.

"With the love I have for you all, I want you to share the company with each other. As you know, I have gone through a lot, and I thank God that I am alive and able to talk with you. I'll share one last thing with you: Life is a risk. We take risks each day that we live It's a part of life, and we have to get used to it. Like I've told you before, nothing in this world is hard unless you want it to be. You can do anything you want, but you must first be confident. The day you stop pursuing what you want, your dream dies. Do you have any questions about what I've just told you or about my decisions?" he asked.

"No, we're satisfied with your decision," Jason said. "We're very happy for Bobby, and we'll work alongside him just as we've been working with you. Congratulations, Bobby."

Jason and Barbara shook Bobby's hand and promised to help him any way they could.

"I want to clarify this," said Solomon. "I gave him this position because he is the oldest male—not because he is any more special. I look at all of you the same, and I have the same respect for your brother as I have for you two—no less and no more. I don't need a board meeting for approval, so, Bobby, please sign this document."

Bobby signed the document, and then Solomon brought out a bottle of champagne. They poured toasts and caroused until the bottle was gone, enjoying the memorable night.

The following day Solomon announced to his employees that he was retiring and introduced them to their new boss. Bobby was happily welcomed by all. That same day Solomon moved his stuff out of the office and turned it over to Bobby. He also gave him permission to make any changes that he wanted to the office, but Bobby told him he planned to keep it just the way it was. This was one of the happiest days of Bobby's life.

The next day Solomon was in Bobby's office with his three children. They were in the middle of a crucial meeting when they heard a soft knock at the office door. He was wondering who it was. "Come inside," he said. But the knocks kept coming at his door. Solomon angrily got up and opened the door. What he saw was shocking. He saw his mother, Clare, standing at the door and grinning at him. Solomon quickly ran to his children screaming, "She's a spirit, she is a spirit." He breathed hard as he ran around searching for a place to hide. "Solomon, it's me your mother. I just got back from Sweden. It took me an entire day to locate your office," she said.

Bobby and Barbara recognized her voice and quickly ran to her as she walked inside the office, calling for Solomon. They happily hugged her and welcomed her. She was so excited to see her grandchildren all grown up. They quickly gave her a seat, but she refused to sit; all she wanted was to see Solomon.

"We thought you were dead," Barbara said.

"Who told you I was dead?" Clare asked.

"Dad told us. Everyone in this community knows that you are dead," Bobby added.

"I am not dead. I was in Sweden, and I've just returned. Wait a minute; is that why Solomon ran when he saw me? she asked.

"Probably," Bobby answered.

Solomon came out from under the desk and stared at his mother. "So you were not dead? Everything that was said about your death was false?" Solomon asked, still prepared to run.

"Dad, Grandma is not dead, and I believe her," Barbara said.

"Thank you God so much for bringing my mother back to me," Solomon said. He hugged her with tears.

It was one of the best days in Solomon's and his children's lives. Clare told them everything that happened. They spent the entire night conversing. Clare was deeply hurt when she heard what happened to her beloved friend, Mrs. Brownell. She couldn't believe that Mr. Carter and her parents actually planned to murder her. She felt betrayed. Clare and Solomon along with her grandchildren were so close. They were now one big happy family. Solomon later bought a house for his mother after she had stayed with him for a year.

Six weeks after Clare moved into her new house, Solomon celebrated his fifty-third birthday at her house, and the entire family was gathered there. Clare tried to make her son's birthday an exciting one.

That night, Solomon took a seat on the white leather couch in Clare's living room. Painted white, the room was sparsely furnished, with a TV, a small bamboo water fountain, a fireplace, and a large painting of Solomon that dominated the east wall. It was tidy and elegant with plenty of space for movement.

Solomon comfortably walked into Clare's kitchen and served himself a cup of coffee. He returned to the living room and sat back down with his children on the white leather couch.

"So what can I do for you my son, since you said you wanted to see me?"

"I have an envelope here for you mom. I wanted to hand it to you personally on this day."

He gave a large, heavy envelope to his mother. She opened it, and the first thing she pulled out was a deed for the land on which her house had been built on the south side of Chicago—before Solomon sold it. There was also a letter addressed to her inside the envelope.

> *Dear Mom,*
> *You are the greatest mother in the world. I love you so much, and I just want to thank you for everything; I mean this from the bottom of my heart. You always told me that life is a risk and that we go through life each day with risk. I know how you felt when Daddy died, and I understood the pain and suffering you went through trying to raise me. You stood by me and watched me grow physically and mentally, and I love you for that. You once told me a story about love, and even though I never knew how powerful the feeling of love was, I thought you were sharing a story about how you met my dad.*
> *When I met my ex-wife, she changed my life, and I now finally understand the true meaning of love. Sometimes I thought her riches gave me more hope and that my dream had been fulfilled—until the day she divorced me and chased me off her property and out of her life.*
> *Please forgive me for all the struggles you underwent for me. When I was in college, you never wanted me to collect student loans, so I watched you work sixty hours a week just to make sure that I had everything I needed for my education. Each time I saw you, you were always smiling and trying to make me happy. It seemed like you were never tired, but I knew you were. I felt sorry for you. Some-*

times I sat in my room and cried for God to help you—to give you some rest, even though we were always broke.

On campus I saw all my friends with expensive clothes and shoes, and they were able to spend more time with their parents. Each time they came to school, they were always smiling, just as you smiled each time you saw me at home. Around this time I started thinking seriously about making fast money so that I could help support us.

Each time I got home from school, our mailbox was full of letters from various collection agencies threatening to make your life miserable for all those credit card loans. I saw how afraid you were to pick up your phone each time it rang, thinking it might be one of the collection agencies or the banks calling for their money.

I used to see how frustrated and depressed you were from all the stress of squeezing time from your job just to take me to listen to motivational speakers and to auto shows. You bought me educational materials so that I would follow a straight and good path toward making my dream a reality.

Always seeing you with headaches and red eyes from exhaustion scared me. So when Ebenezer gave me that great opportunity to get rich, I decided to take a shot at making money and give school a break. I reasoned that once I was comfortable, I would go back to school to finish my education.

You knew that I had always wanted to get rich, and you thought that I was working very hard toward that dream during the time I was away. But instead I was always in trouble with the law. I met some good people and some bad people along the way. I learned so much from the street, but I realized I had nothing to show for my struggles. The money you gave me changed my life; it made me the man I am today.

When I received the money you left with your letter at Grandma's house, I went back to New York, and I could see God's light shining in front of me toward my future. It showed me the path you wanted me to take. I then understood that you had been saving your hard-earned money for me, and I knew you were happy when you realized how prosperous I'd become from that money. I know that you are proud of me and that you always have been.

I did online studies, and I finally was able to obtain my master's degree in education. I have all of my documents in this envelope. I know it will make you happy to see them. I also bought back your former house, and all the documents are in your name. I put you down as the owner of my businesses, and I have put my accounts in your name. Everything I own has been transferred to you because I believe that you are the rightful owner.

I'm happy because I was able to see and taste the power of money; it changed my life and made everything easy for me. It's hard to explain what money can help you accomplish. I have donated seventy-five thousand dollars to the Breast Cancer Society of America and the Spinal Cord Foundation. I pray that my children will go through what I'm going through right now.

I have enclosed a picture of me when I was a boy growing up. I love you, and I will always love you.

May God richly bless you for having been my mother, and I will be there to celebrate the next Thanksgiving and Mother's Day with you. I love you, Mom, and I thank you for everything.

Your loving son,
Solomon Jensen

When Clare finished reading the letter out loud, she shook as hot tears of joy rolled from her eyes. She drank some water and rested for couple of minutes before taking out the other items from the envelope. Solomon's children eyes were also filled with tears.

"I love you too, my son." She looked at Solomon and smiled. "Thank you for been my son and my best friend. I am so proud to be your mother and I will always love you. Thank you."

www.ingramcontent.com/pod-product-compliance
Lightning Source LLC
LaVergne TN
LVHW051543070426
835507LV00021B/2388

Highest Praise for *I LOVE YOU, MOM*

"SUSPENSE NOVEL THAT WILL HAVE READERS STAYING UP AT NIGHT WITH LIGHT ON."
-BOOKREPORTER.COM

"A FAST-PACED THRILLER."
-DAVID BALDACCI

"A PSYCHOLOGICAL THRILLER OF THE FIRST ORDER."
-ICE-T

"WILL KEEP YOU ON THE EDGE OF YOUR SEAT. HIGHLY RECOMMENDED."
-ARLENA DEAN

"ONE THING FOR SURE...HE LOVE HIS MOM."
-LITERARY COMMUNITY

"RIVETING PSYCHOLOGICAL SUSPENSE."
-*Will smith*

"Dr. Carter Brown's thriller explores the turbulent life of a man whose only constant is his unwavering love for his mother."
-KIRKUS REVIEWS